MW01033236

What others are saying about this book:

This is the most practical, realistic, and helpful book on the subject of witnessing that I have read in forty years of pastoral ministry. It will be used by the Lord to free many people who have been reticent to share their faith.

Rev. Dewey Corder,
Pastor, Central Baptist Church, Trussville, AL
Former President, Alabama Baptist Convention (SBC)

Evangelism for the Tongue-Tied delivers a fresh, down-to-earth plan that will help untie the tongues of everyday Christians. The insights on biblical, evangelistic prayer alone are worth the price of the book. Put these principles into practice, and you will share your faith!

Walt Day,
Chapel Leader, New England Patriots and Boston Red Sox

If we are to see a spiritual change in our country, it must come from ordinary Christians confronting unbelievers with the wonderful news of salvation. Evangelism for the Tongue-Tied is informative and inspiring, and it makes evangelistic principles easy for the "ordinary" Christian. Every church could benefit from studying it.

Ken Speakman,
Retired Director, International Division, Gideons International

As a tongue-tied missionary in the midst of African animism, I am reminded by Chap's book that it is God who will be opening the doors for people to hear about Jesus' power, love, and righteousness. I just have to ask for open doors, look for what He's doing, jump on board, and enjoy the ride.

Brian Schrag,
Wycliffe Bible Translators, Yaoundé, Cameroon

One of the greatest barriers to effective witness comes at the moment a Christian wants to break the ice and speak about Christ to a friend. Evangelism for the Tongue-Tied equips the Christian to break through that barrier. This book is gentle in tone, practical in its advice, and biblically informed throughout. Ordinary Christians can lead a life of fruitful witness. I highly recommend it!

Tim Zulker,
Director, The Philip Center, Rhode Island

I have never read an evangelism book that was as accessible as this one. I sense that this would be a great help to all the families in our church to help move us to the next level in evangelism.

Craig Noll,
Elder, Davisville House Church, North Kingstown, RI

You have to have this published! I would use this immediately in one of our Sunday school classes.

Rev. Phil Curtis,
Pastor, Exeter Chapel, Exeter, RI

This book is going to be used of the Lord. It is "right on" and the answer for Christians who have a burden for the lost.

Richard Nooney,
Former State President, MA/RI Gideons

Evangelism
for the
Tongue-Tied

Evangelism

for the

Tongue-Tied

HOW ANYONE CAN TELL OTHERS ABOUT JESUS

Chap Bettis

A Division of WINEPRESS PUBLISHING

© 2004 by Chap Bettis. All rights reserved.

Printed in the United States of America

Packaged by Pleasant Word, a division of WinePress Publishing, PO Box 428, Enumclaw, WA 98022. The views expressed or implied in this work do not necessarily reflect those of Pleasant Word, a division of WinePress Publishing. Ultimate design, content, and editorial accuracy of this work are the responsibilities of the author.

No part of this publication may be reproduced, stored in a retrieval system, or transmitted in any way by any means—electronic, mechanical, photocopy, recording, or otherwise—without the prior permission of the copyright holder, except as provided by USA copyright law.

In this book, the author has placed certain words from the scriptural quotations in italics without individually marking each instance with such words as "italics mine." The reader should be aware, however, that these italics are not found in the original texts but are added by the author for reasons of emphasis and clarity.

Unless otherwise noted, all Scriptures are taken from the Holy Bible, New International Version, Copyright © 1973, 1978, 1984 by the International Bible Society. Used by permission of Zondervan Publishing House. The "NIV" and "New International Version" trademarks are registered in the United States Patent and Trademark Office by International Bible Society.

ISBN 1-4141-0141-4
Library of Congress Catalog Card Number: 2004101518

To Sharon,
my partner in the gospel

Contents

Acknowledgments

I am indebted to the following people for their contributions to this process. The elders of Lincoln Christian Fellowship—Dan, Steve, and Greg—have been extremely patient with me over the years. I could not ask for better teammates in the ministry of the gospel. The same is true for the members of LCF. You have patiently endured my experiments and followed the elders' leadership. Thank you for letting me use your stories.

My parents have made many sacrifices and have given much encouragement. The same is true for Sharon's parents, who have been like parents to me and not like in-laws. I am so thankful for your input into my life.

Other individuals deserve mention for their contributions. Ruth Allderige was helpful in encouraging me to begin writing and in her editorial advice. Dennis Reiter shared his personal insight and helped me with vocational coaching. Craig Noll also gave editorial help. Eric Holter and the folks at Newfangled Graphics have put together a superior web site to support and enhance this book. Thanks to Joe Tatulli for his help on the cover concept. Dr. Thom Rainer, Tim Zulker, and Bruce Dreisbach also gave insightful comments.

Dick Scoggins, David Gadoury, and Phil Curtis have all been mentors and models. I have enjoyed serving together with you over the years and look forward to the future. In addition, Mike Buffi, Steve Abbott, Dennis Hardiman, Kent Enos, and Jim Frost all keep teaching me new insights regarding evangelism.

Finally, but most importantly, a big thank you to my family. Kara, Chapman, Rebekah, and Nate, you have patiently endured me talking this project to death. You also let me go several times so I could finish it. And, Sharon, you are my true partner in the gospel and an example of a believer who reaches out to others.

Introduction

Star athletes are enthralling. Adults marvel at their performance while children seek to imitate them. How did they rise to this level of achievement? Part of the answer lies in their hard work. But star athletes also excel because of natural gifting and talent. No matter how hard the rest of us try, we will never have enough natural ability to achieve their level of play.

What about the Rest of Us?

For years, I have read and listened to the stories of gifted evangelists. After the initial encouragement, I watched my own experiences fall far short. The gap between their experience and mine was discouraging. But during those years, I also began to learn evangelistic principles that worked for me, a tongue-tied Christian. In talking with others, I discovered that many Christians shared my plight. They wanted desperately to share their faith with co-workers and friends. But, like me, they didn't know how to bring the subject up. As a result, they felt guilty.

If these biblical principles can work for me, I know they can work for you. These principles are not new. What is new is the arrangement and presentation of these simple skills together. There are plenty of books written to help us do a better job of presenting the gospel once we are on the subject with someone else. But there aren't a lot of resources to help us overcome the barriers and bring up the subject in the first place. Scripture says that if we sow generously we will reap generously. These principles will help you sow the word of God generously. All of us are called to sow. Some may also be privileged to reap.

God Uses Ordinary Christians

My goal in the following pages is to make evangelistic principles simple for the ordinary Christian. It may be more effective to train those with the spiritual gift of evangelism. But those of us who are tongue-tied miss out on the fun. Ordinary Christians, properly trained, can have extraordinary joy. Perhaps you work in an office or factory or attend school and you cannot ever seem to bring up your faith. Or perhaps you don't want to start sharing your faith because you don't know what you would say after you do.

This book is intentionally simple but not simplistic. My goal is to produce a readable handbook for busy people. As a result, this resource is not comprehensive. Other more comprehensive resources are listed in appendix A.

Some Assumptions to Save Time

In writing this book, I have made a number of assumptions in order to save time. I have not spent time urging you to live a life that will match your words. Your character in your family and work must match your words. That is not to say you must be sinless, but you must not have a life-dominating sin that will negate your words. If your life does not match your words, put the book down and work on your life first.

Nor have I spent time answering every objection non-Christians will have. Other books do a fine job of helping with that. See appendix A or www.tonguetied.org for a list of helpful resources.

In addition, I have not taken room to talk about what to do when a person receives Christ. There are many excellent books on following up new Christians. Again, appendix A has a fine list of resources.

All of these things are important. But most of us need to just start talking about Jesus. This is a book to help us *start*.

People Helping People

In a healthy church, adults are reaching out to other adults. Yes, children need to be evangelized. But if you win the parents (and especially the fathers), you will win the children. Many churches focus on reaching children with the gospel. But adults also need to be talking to their peers. There is a vitality and excitement in a church where adults are sharing their faith with other adults.

God will give you a role in that proclamation. You *can* proclaim the good news of Jesus Christ to the people God has placed in your life.

CHAPTER 1

You Can Tell Others about Jesus

Meet David, a deacon in First Community Church. David became a Christian in college when he met two Christians taking a spiritual survey on the campus green. He grew quickly, absorbing everything he was taught and excitedly telling his classmates about Jesus Christ. He took part in dorm outreach events and saw others put their faith in Christ. But now, twenty years later, things have changed. David's faith has slowed down even while his life has sped up. Work, family, and church responsibilities consume all his time and energy. David rarely shares with anyone in the large company where he works. He can't remember the last time he shared his faith. Even though he is surrounded by non-Christians at work, David can't seem to recapture the boldness he had in college. And when Pastor Bob speaks of telling others about Jesus, David feels guilty but helpless. The only way he knows to rationalize this guilt is by telling himself that he's just not an evangelist. That explanation makes him feel a little better.

Meet Nichole, a college sophomore. Nichole became a Christian in David's church when she was a child. In her teen years, she attended a church-wide evangelism-training program. As suggested by the program, she prayed for one other teen to come to faith through her that year. She never saw that prayer answered and, as a result, grew discouraged about sharing her faith. Between this discouragement and her intellectual questioning, her faith faltered. Now in college, she has begun meeting with other earnest Christians. Her questions have been answered, and she has grown excited again about sharing her faith. But Nichole finds it difficult to relate to non-Christians. The evangelism techniques she is being taught feel forced. Any attempt to write her testimony seems like a complete flop because she received Christ when she was five. No other college student can relate to her background. Frustrated, she finds herself wondering if she will ever learn to share her faith with others.

Meet Pastor Bob, the shepherd of David's and Nichole's church. When Bob became a Christian in his twenties, Jesus completely changed his life. At first, he told everyone he met about Jesus. A few in his family also professed Christ, although most mocked his new faith. But Bob was serious about this new life. He sold his house and began attending seminary. Now a church leader, he finds few chances to witness except in his official role as a pastor. Between preparing sermons, counseling, and leading meetings, he rarely takes time to interact with non-Christians. Looking over his congregation, he realizes how few of his people share their faith during the week. These are good people who love Jesus Christ and sincerely desire to tell others about him. But they don't know how. Many times he's preached sermons on being a bold witness, but he's seen few results. He knows his congregation needs more. But what? Besides, Pastor Bob has a hard time asking his people to do something he's not doing.

Three people. Different lives, but one problem. When it comes to sharing their faith, they all feel tongue-tied.

Hope for the Tongue-Tied

Because you are reading this book, I can already tell we have three things in common. First, you desire that our Lord use you in spreading the good news of salvation. Second, when it comes to sharing your faith, you feel tongue-tied, inept, and awkward. Third, in spite of this awkwardness, you still desire to grow in sharing your faith.

We know that there is great joy and excitement in proclaiming the salvation that Christ freely offers. There is even greater joy in watching and helping a new Christian be born. We are right to long after this privilege. Paul wanted Philemon to proclaim his faith. "I pray that you may be active in sharing your faith, so that you will have a full understanding of every good thing we have in Christ" (Philemon 6). As this verse demonstrates, there is a connection between witnessing and a healthy Christian life. Paul Little has said, "Witnessing is one of the keys to spiritual health. I like to call it the fizz in the Pepsi of the Christian life, because it puts sparkle and verve into our faith."[1]

The witnessing Christian is a healthy Christian. Evangelism is a means of God's grace to *our* souls. When we share our faith, we are focused on things that really matter—the growth of God's kingdom and a person's eternal destiny. As we talk with unbelievers and learn of their problems, it helps put our own problems in perspective. A witnessing Christian will also spend less time bickering and fighting other Christians. Joe Aldrich observes:

> Many in the church are like caged hunting dogs. With no birds to hunt, they spend their time nipping, scrapping, and fighting each other. Turned loose to fulfill their destiny, to pursue their quarry, to fulfill their great commission, they stop biting and fighting.[2]

However, we face formidable barriers when trying to proclaim Christ. We live in a secular time when many people think that religious things are best left in church. Organized religion is seen as quaint and irrelevant to the needs and problems of everyday life. We experience daily the fact that "no one seeks God" (Romans 3:11). Few bring up spiritual things unprompted.

Can You Identify?

In addition to this secularization, we are well aware of our own inadequacies. If we do try to share our faith, we don't know where to begin. Our palms start to sweat, our mouths become dry, and our minds turn to mush. In a word, we become *tongue-tied,* that is, "deprived of speech or power of distinct articulation; made speechless, silent, unable to speak freely."[3]

That definition aptly described me until I began to understand the principles presented in the following pages. This book has grown out of my own struggles, victories, and setbacks and is written as an encouragement to others who have the same verbal struggles.

Most gifted evangelists have had a dramatic adult conversion. They also seem naturally skilled in dealing with people and know exactly what to say and when to say it.

I, on the other hand, don't have a dramatic testimony. I grew up in a Christian home and accepted the Lord when I was around eight years old. I was not saved dramatically as an adult from drugs or alcohol or some other worldly bondage. Actually, I find it difficult to relate to the inner emptiness that some experienced before they came to Christ as an adult.

In addition, I'm not naturally an extrovert or a gifted conversationalist. I have to think about what I am going to say ahead of time. When I began dating the woman I soon would marry, I would write down topics to talk about or questions to ask her so the conversation wouldn't lag.

Furthermore, I don't think well on my feet. When placed in a conflict, I'm usually on the receiving end of the barbed comments and can never think of a snappy retort—until two hours later. Then I know exactly what I should have said!

Are any of these characteristics true of you? Have you desired to share your faith but felt inadequate because you don't have a dramatic conversion story or because you are not naturally an extrovert? The gap between what we perceive gifted evangelists to be and the way God has made us can be discouraging. The call to evangelize can seem like an impossible command. When we listen to the stories of gifted evangelists, it is easy to be filled with guilt and despair.

Current Evangelistic Helps

If we survey the current evangelistic helps, we find that most fall into one of two categories. On the one hand, there are excellent books written by gifted evangelists. These books inspire us with their stories and instruct us with their principles. But often our own experience falls far short of the stories described. If they relay a story of sharing the gospel on an airplane, then we try something similar and fail miserably. So we give up, concluding that we are not gifted evangelists and that the Lord will never use us to share our faith.

On the other hand, we have evangelistic helps that consist of structured programs. These programs usually involve a script to memorize and a structured time and place to witness, such as the home of a recent church visitor. These programs have been helpful in aiding many of us who are tongue-tied. Without these programs we would not know how to share our faith at all. However, because these programs are so structured, we often are still not equipped to share our faith at other times. While officially "witnessing" we are an effective bearer of the good news. But in the day-to-day, we have difficulty sharing the gospel with friends and co-workers.

Yet even with these resources, less than half of Christians have shared their faith with anyone in the past twelve months. No wonder North American church growth is stagnant. But the good news of this book is that by understanding and practicing a few simple principles, you can enjoy a lifetime of sharing your faith.

I don't know whether God will give you the privilege of leading someone to Christ. But if you will follow the principles presented in these chapters, I do know he will give you the privilege of speaking about him. If you came to Christ as a child or don't have a dramatic conversion story, then this book will be of help to you. If you are not a gifted communicator, then these principles will aid you.

The Need for All to Share

The need for all of us to share our faith has never been greater. More than half the people who have ever lived in human history are alive today. Stated another way, the total number of people who have been alive from creation until today is less than the number of beating hearts at this very second. There are simply not enough evangelists, pastors, and missionaries to reach everyone with a clear presentation of the gospel. For some people, the closest they will ever come to the gospel is you.

Not only is the need great in terms of numbers, but the stakes that hang in the balance are great as well. C. S. Lewis states it this way:

It is a serious thing to live in a society of possible gods and goddesses, to remember that the dullest and most uninteresting person you can talk to may one day be a creature which, if you saw it now, you would be strongly tempted to worship, or else a horror or corruption such as you now meet, if at all, only in a nightmare. All day long we are, in some degree, helping each other to one or other of these possible destinations. . . . There are no *ordinary* people. You have never talked to a mere mortal. Nations, cultures, arts, civilizations—these are mortal, and their life is to ours as the life of a gnat. But it is immortals whom we joke with, work with, marry, snub, and exploit—immortal horrors or everlasting splendours.[4]

So how can we who are tongue-tied Christians become more effective at sharing our faith? Is there really hope that an ordinary Christian can grow in this area? Yes, yes, a thousand times yes! Before proceeding, though, let's clear our minds of some myths.

Myth 1—Professional Evangelists Are Most Effective

The first myth to dispel is that most people come to the Lord through well-known evangelists. When someone mentions effective evangelists, we think of Billy Graham or Luis Palau. But most people who come to the Lord as teenagers and adults come through the witness and encouragement of a friend. Actually, to your friends, you are the most effective evangelist they can have. A survey from the Institute of American Church Growth found that 75 to 90 percent of those who come to faith do so through a friend or acquaintance who explains the gospel to them one-to-one. This is the method God blesses!

Take an informal survey in your own church. Who has become a Christian as an adult? How did those people first come in contact with the gospel? What did it take for them to give themselves to Christ? You will find that most people come to the Lord through friends, relatives, and relationships at a local level. God has designed evangelism to work this way.

Myth 2—We Must Win Them to Christ

The second myth to reject is that we have not been successful if the person does not receive Christ. Converting the human heart is the Holy Spirit's job. Our job is to proclaim the message clearly and winsomely. If we have been able to proclaim Christ, we have been victorious. J. I. Packer succinctly states it this way, "While we must always remember that it is our responsibility to proclaim salvation, we must never forget that it is God who saves."[5]

Unfortunately, some have put all the responsibility for conversion of the human heart upon us. In addition, we are trained by hearing all the "success" stories. In the process, we overlook the sowing that must happen first. Jesus said that the farmer went out to sow the word (Mark 4:14). Our responsibility is to sow the word. But many of the resources don't teach us to sow, they teach us to harvest. In that same parable, we notice that the reaction to the gospel does not depend on the sower; it depends on the nature of the soil. Our job is to sow the word generously. We must let God determine the reactions. He promises some will reject it, some will receive it with joy and fall away, but still others will receive the message and produce great fruit. This knowledge can help us relax and concentrate on our responsibility. Michael Horton reminds us:

> We know that, in the final analysis, only God's electing, redeeming grace, and not Madison Avenue or the latest fads of pop psychology, will bring lasting reconciliation between humans and God. With this knowledge we can be more comfortable with the biblical message and biblical methods. We can approach unbelievers as human beings rather than targets, consumers, numbers and converts.[6]

Every time we sow the word and engage an unbeliever in thinking about eternal things, we have been victorious.

Myth 3—Evangelism Cannot Be Learned

The third myth to destroy is that because we are not gifted as an evangelist, we cannot learn anything about evangelism. Stated another way, we often believe that evangelism is something you either have or you don't have. But that simply is not true. Just because I am not talented enough to play professional football does not mean I cannot play a pick-up game with my friends or my children.

Evangelism is a skill. Evangelism can be broken down into different skills to be learned and mastered. Anyone who has ever participated in a sport can understand the process. When I watch Olympic gymnasts compete, I am dumbfounded. As an outsider to gymnastics, I have no idea how the athletes develop the ability to perform these moves. But I have played basketball. So when I watch a basketball game, I know that the athlete's fluid play is the result of mastering many different skills. Whether at the YMCA or in the NBA, every basketball player works on skills like dribbling, passing, shooting, and rebounding. What looks mysterious to the outsider is really the result of mastering many individual skills.

Evangelism is similar. When put together by a gifted evangelist, the skills needed are confusing and overwhelming to the rest of us. But if we will break the skills down into learnable pieces and grow in each area, then we will be well on the way to sharing our faith. These skills will not be mastered overnight. But if we persevere in developing our abilities little by little, we can and will see progress.

The Four Steps to Presenting the Gospel

There really are just four different steps to becoming more proficient in presenting the gospel. We will be looking at these skills in the following chapters.

- Step 1 is *praying biblical prayers* from Colossians 4:2–6. This will be covered in chapter 2.
- Step 2 is *building genuine relationships with unbelievers*. Chapters 3 and 4 will guide you to build relationships with unbelievers that can lead to the gospel.
- Step 3 is *transitioning the conversation to spiritual things* when God opens the door. Chapters 5, 6, and 7 will train you in bringing the gospel into your situation. Handling a few responses is covered in chapter 8.
- Step 4 is *using God-blessed resources* that will aid you in proclaiming the gospel. Suggestions are made for these in chapter 9.

Once broken down, these steps are really quite simple. If I can learn them, then so can you.

Moses, Our Encouragement

After Moses met God in the burning bush, God gave him the assignment of bringing his people out of bondage. But Moses argued with the Lord.

Moses said to the Lord, "O Lord, I have never been eloquent, neither in the past nor since you have spoken to your servant. I am slow of speech and tongue." The Lord said to him, "Who gave man his mouth? Who makes him deaf or dumb? Who gives him sight or makes him blind? Is it not I, the Lord? Now go, *I will help you speak and will teach you what to say.*" (Exodus 4:10–12)

The Lord has given us an assignment as well. We are to speak about our Lord, knowing that he will use us to lead men and women out of the bondage of sin. In the past, we have not gone because we are slow of speech and tongue. But who made you the way you are? Is it not the Lord? In spite of your slowness of·speech, he promises to help you speak and to teach you what to say. With that promise in mind, are you ready to obey his command? If so, then turn the page and let's begin!

CHAPTER 2

Praying Effective Evangelistic Prayers

What comes to your mind when you think of evangelistic prayer? Whenever I ask people "What is the last evangelistic prayer the Lord answered in your life?" the answers I hear are similar. A few people recount wonderful stories of friends or relatives finally coming to know the Lord, often after years and years of praying. These answers to prayer are encouraging to all of us. Many people, however, simply stare at me. They rarely have had an evangelistic prayer answered, and as a result, they have given up praying for others.

Am I Praying Correctly?

Perhaps one reason we see so few answers to evangelistic prayers is because we have never been taught how to pray such prayers. Maybe it has never crossed your mind that God might give you evangelistic prayers that can result in regular answers. But he has.

I am not here to add one more religious duty to your already busy life. Rather, I want to invite you on a personal adventure of praying evangelistic requests that God will regularly answer. The most important change that a tongue-tied Christian can make is to change his or her evangelistic praying. If our tongues are to become untied, it is not because we will have learned a technique from this or any other book. Our tongues will become untied as we cry out to the one who made us the way we are. Colossians 4:2–4 provides the help we need.

> Devote yourselves to prayer, being watchful and thankful. And pray for us, too, that *God may open a door for our message*, so that we may proclaim the mystery of Christ, for which I am in chains. *Pray that I may proclaim it clearly*, as I should.

Pray for Open Doors

What did Paul understand that we don't? Paul wrote the book of Colossians from Rome after he had completed three highly success-ful missionary journeys. In spite of his successes, the apostle Paul still felt the need for the prayers of others. Specifically, he felt the need for prayer that God would open a door for the message. Paul understood that for him to proclaim Christ, God would have to open a door. God would open that door only as his people asked him.

We must understand this truth. Our job is to proclaim Christ. But we cannot proclaim Christ until God opens a door. God will not make an opportunity until we ask him. Therefore, like Paul, we need to pray for *open doors*. The process looks like this:

Our job		God's job		Our job
Pray for	→	Open the	→	Proclaim
open doors		door		Christ

Many are discouraged in sharing their faith because they don't understand this supernatural process. Some programs put all the re-sponsibility on proclaiming the message, whether or not there is an opportunity. Other books written by gifted evangelists describe them taking advantage of opportunities you and I would never see.

The key for the tongue-tied Christian is persistent prayer that God will open opportunities for the message. When he answers, we can walk through those doors confidently and graciously, knowing that he gave us the opportunity. When we try to pry open an evangelistic door, it usually results in hard feelings on the other person's part and a bad experience on our part.

When tongue-tied Christians understand this insight from Scripture, there is often an immediate answer to prayer. After one presentation I made of this teaching, I received this e-mail:

> What you had to share was both incredibly relevant and fruitful. It has already borne fruit in a woman Ellie has been sharing with. She was praying for open doors for one friend and literally five minutes later this friend called her and asked her to get together. When we pray in God's will, things happen.

I have often prayed that God would open a way for the message. He has been faithful to answer that prayer. I regularly have sensed God's Spirit telling me that there was an opening in front of me. And then I had a choice to walk through that door or not. Some of those answers have been dramatic. Other answers have been more commonplace. But prayer for God to open a way is vital. As you begin praying, you will suddenly see divine "coincidences." But these coincidences only happen to those who pray.

If you truly understand the need to pray for open doors, evangelistic prayer will become an exciting adventure. Now, instead of praying by rote for someone's salvation over and over, you are actually inviting God to invade your world and the circumstances in your life and make an opening for his message. God will answer that prayer before you know it!

Pray for Ourselves

Not only do we need to be devoted to praying for open doors; we also need to be devoted to praying for *ourselves*. Even after his previous successes, the apostle Paul knew he needed prayer that he might proclaim the mystery of Christ *clearly*. "Pray that I may proclaim it clearly, as I should" (Colossians 4:4). At the end of Ephesians, which he wrote at the same time, Paul asks for prayer that he would proclaim the message *fearlessly*. "Pray that I may declare [the mystery of the gospel] fearlessly, as I should" (Ephesians 6:20).

These are two of the most basic and effective prayers we can pray for ourselves. First, we need to pray to proclaim the message of Christ clearly, so that the unbeliever can understand. Second, we need to pray that we will overcome our fear of rejection and that we will proclaim the gospel fearlessly. If we have presented the message clearly and fearlessly, God has answered prayer, and we have done our job.

Pray to proclaim Christ clearly. Why do we need to proclaim Christ clearly? For most people, the true message of Jesus Christ is still a mystery. Many don't understand who Jesus really is and what he did on the cross. They have all sorts of wrong views. Many people are rejecting a caricatured Jesus from their childhood or a view of Jesus they have gathered from television or magazine articles. If pressed, most would say that Jesus was a great religious teacher. His message, like all great religious men, was to love one another.

Our job is to counter this misunderstanding with the truth of the gospel. The proclamation of truth is the only way that wrong or inadequate views will be challenged. Our responsibility is to make sure that our proclamation is as clear as possible. We cannot control our listeners' reaction to the message, but we can offer an intelligible message to which they can respond. When we have explained Christ clearly, this prayer has been answered.

When God answers this prayer for clarity, what we say will be understandable. It does not mean we have to proclaim the whole message at once. But what we do say must be crystal clear. I know well the feeling of stumbling over my words, trying to explain some part of the gospel. During my explanation, I realized that my words were not clear to me, so how could they be clear to the person I was talking with?

Pray to proclaim Christ fearlessly. Likewise, we need to pray for ourselves that we will declare the message fearlessly. Fear of rejection is still the number one barrier to sharing the gospel consistently. The solution is to pray for boldness.

After God had begun teaching me to pray differently, I recognized him opening a door in a conversation at work. As I stood in that co-worker's cubical I was outwardly continuing the conversation, but inwardly I was wrestling with whether to bring up the gospel. In the end, my sinful flesh won, and I left without speaking to her about the gospel. As I went back to the Scriptures in despair, I rediscovered Ephesians 6:20. It gave me great encouragement that the apostle Paul, after proclaiming the message fearlessly to the Roman rulers and the Jews in Jerusalem and Asia Minor, still felt needy enough to ask for prayer to proclaim the message fearlessly. If he needed prayer in this area, how much more did I need it!

Don't misinterpret this prayer for fearlessness as a prayer for arrogance, insensitivity, or rudeness. Later, we will be talking about how to speak to unbelievers. Unfortunately, some Christians equate speaking fearlessly with speaking harshly and insensitively. But Scripture says we are to speak with "gentleness and respect" (1 Peter 3:15). An answer to this prayer means we boldly take advantage of doors the Lord opens. It also means we say the hard things that Jesus said in a loving and humble manner. It does not mean we are rude.

Pray Obstinately

Finally, we need to pray *obstinately*. God instructs us, "Devote yourselves to prayer, being watchful and thankful" (Colossians 4:2). The battle for people's souls is waged in the heavenly realms, and the proclamation of the gospel is opposed by the devil. If the gospel is going to go forward, it is because we are on our knees in prayer. As individuals, as families, as small groups, and as churches, we must be continuously praying that the Lord would open doors for the message and that we would declare the gospel clearly and fearlessly.

Being watchful and thankful. But this command to pray is not a repetitive duty. The rest of the verse says we are to be watchful and thankful. Watchful and thankful for what? We are to be watchful and thankful for regular answers to these prayers. That's right—we should expect to see regular answers to our evangelistic prayers! When we don't see regular answers, evangelistic prayer can become a rote duty. When we see frequent answers, prayer becomes a supernatural adventure.

God can answer your evangelistic prayers entirely apart from whether or not people come to Christ. By opening the door for you to proclaim the message, God has answered evangelistic prayer. By making you bolder than you were last time, God has answered evangelistic prayer; and by helping you proclaim Christ more clearly, God has answered evangelistic prayer. We can see regular answers to these prayers, regardless of the response of the ones with whom we talk.

Rather than praying "hope-so" prayers, we are to co-work and cooperate with God by praying smaller prayers where we will recognize answers. As we learn to pray in the Spirit, asking him what to pray for, we will see many answered prayers. Someone coming to Christ is usually the result of many answered prayers for opportunity, clarity, curiosity, wisdom for the next step, insight into the person's heart, and so forth. When we just pray for someone's salvation, we put all the responsibility on God. When we begin to pray for ourselves, we realize that we also have some responsibility to act.

As tongue-tied Christians, we often desire to pray instead of act. But this Scripture commands us to pray that God will enable *us* to act. If we ask God to do all the work of salvation and refuse to do our part, this evangelistic partnership will not succeed. If we don't ask God to do anything and rely only on ourselves, this adventure will fail. But if we ask God to do his part and to enable us to do our part, it will succeed.

Other Ways to Pray

Having emphasized the need to pray obstinately for open doors and ourselves, let's bring some balance. There are other ways we can pray evangelistically.

First, in addition to praying these prayers from Colossians 4:2–4, we can also pray for ability to carry out the *commands* in verses 5 and 6. These would include prayer for insight in how to act wisely toward outsiders and how to make the most of every opportunity. In addition, we can pray for gracious conversations and insight into how to answer each one. We will be discussing these different commands in the following chapters.

Second, we can pray for insight into the *strongholds* that keep our unbelieving friends from coming to Jesus. "The god of this age has blinded the minds of unbelievers, so that they cannot see the light of the gospel of the glory of Christ, who is the image of God" (2 Corinthians 4:4). For different people there are different hindrances to the gospel. For some, the hindrance may be bitterness at God for a past tragedy. For others, it may be pride in learning. For still others, a hindrance may be their love of money. Ask God to give you insight into their particular cause of blindness. Once you have insight into their cause of blindness, you can begin to pray against it.

Third, we can pray for God to guide us to *someone in need*. God often uses pain and need to gain the attention of unbelievers and believers alike. And God often uses his people to minister to that pain in unbelievers. However, if we are too absorbed in our own lives, we will miss these appointments. Praying for God to guide us to someone in need will make us sensitive to the Holy Spirit and others. God will answer that prayer quickly.

As a related prayer, we can ask to be guided to *someone in whom God is already working*. Jesus made clear that one work of the Holy Spirit is to convict the world of sin, righteousness, and judgment (John 16:8–11). We can be confident knowing that this invisible work of the Holy Spirit in people's hearts is constantly occurring. We just need to pray that he would guide us to those people.

Fourth, we can pray for an *unbeliever's prayer request*. When an unbeliever shares a need with us, often we don't know what to say. An excellent response is an offer to pray. We will be talking about this again in chapter 7. Our prayer for the person invites God's special blessing upon them. It also gives us a chance to follow up with them in the future. And remember, if we promise to pray, we should keep our promise.

Practical Helps

How can we make sure we are devoted to evangelistic prayer? Daily pressures can easily crowd out the best intentions. If we devote ourselves to evangelistic prayer, it will be because we have set up a realistic plan with realistic accountability. The following three methods will be helpful in keeping you on track.

The first help is a *physical reminder* to pray regularly. This reminder can be as simple as a notation in your prayer journal, a note on your bureau, or a note at your place of work. Another reminder could be the act of placing a gospel pamphlet in your appointment book each day. Or you could use a devotional prayer guide to help you stay on track. Houses of Prayer Everywhere has two helpful resources. *Praying the Lord's Prayer for Neighbors* is a twenty-eight-day devotional guide that helps you learn to pray the Lord's Prayer for yourself and your neighbors. *Developing a Prayer-Care-Share Lifestyle* is a fifteen-week devotional book that will guide your evangelistic prayer time and will remind you to pray. These physical booklets, kept with your Bible for devotions, will remind you to devote yourself to prayer.

Praying through your day's appointments and errands will help you mentally walk through the day. As you do this, you can invite the Holy Spirit to open doors for the message at each of these places. Or you can invite the Holy Spirit to bring people to you. One of our church's elders was saved as a college student by a Christian woman who did just that. Though homebound due to an illness, she asked the Lord to send someone to her that she could tell about Jesus. Steve knocked on her door that day ready to make a sales pitch to her. Instead, a little later, he was praying to receive Christ.

A second help that can keep you devoted to prayer is *attendance at a small group meeting*. Whether a Sunday school class or a mid-week home group, almost all small groups have a prayer time. If a group is not reaching out, this prayer time can become ingrown and stale. How much better to use this occasion to bring up biblical evangelistic prayer for open doors, clarity, and fearlessness. Imagine the encouragement all would receive if each time you heard of open doors the Lord gave during the past week. Even if the Lord did not answer your own prayers that week, it will encourage you to hear the reports of others. Not only will this regular meeting remind you to pray, but it will also remind you to be watchful for answers. These regular times of prayer will help keep you accountable.

A third practical help to keep your evangelistic prayer life on track is *covenanting with one or two others* in your church. "Two are better than one . . . if one falls down, his friend can help him up" (Ecclesiastes 4:9–10). Perhaps you know of a few others who are burdened for evangelism in your fellowship. Just a short talk with them every Sunday before or after church can be a quick accountability group. To begin with, try committing yourself to pray once a week for ninety days and see what God does through your prayers.

The Lord Will Answer Biblical Prayer

The most important part of this passage in Colossians is "being watchful and thankful." If you are watching for answers to prayer, and if you are ready to be thankful for answers to prayer, then you are on the road to praying well. You are going to enter into the adventure of evangelistic prayer. Take confidence in the fact that these are biblical prayers. God himself has revealed these to us as ways he desires us to pray. He will answer these prayers.

If you have difficulty seeing regular answers to these prayers, you need to ask the Lord to show you the reason. Good prayer requires the *mouth* to speak to God. But it also involves the *ear* in hearing what the Spirit is saying to us and the *eye* in watching for answers. While keeping your *mouth* open in intercession also keep your *ears* open in listening to the Spirit and your *eyes* open in watching for answers.

Praying well is just the beginning of the adventure. We must do more than pray, but we cannot do more until we have prayed.

For Thought, Discussion, and Action

- Begin praying these prayers from Colossians 4:2–6 during your devotional time.
- Share this passage with your Sunday school class, small group, prayer circle, prayer partner, etc. and begin praying this passage on a regular basis. Share the answers as you see them.
- Order *Developing a Prayer-Care-Share Lifestyle* or *Praying the Lord's Prayer for Neighbors* at www.tonguetied.org.

CHAPTER 3

Building Genuine Relationships with Unbelievers

A very timid gentleman had heard his pastor preach over and over again about boldness in sharing Jesus with the lost. This man began to pray for the Lord to give him a sign as to when he was to witness. The next day he got on the bus to ride to work. Just as he sat down, the biggest, meanest-looking man he had ever seen got on the bus, walked down the aisle, and sat next to him. When the man sat down, he began to weep. He turned to the timid man and said, "I'm lost and don't know how to be saved. I need someone to tell me about Jesus. Are you a Christian?" The timid gentleman immediately bowed his head and prayed, "Lord, is this a sign?"

Just as in this story, tongue-tied Christians often want God to do all the work. Instead, God commands us to take an additional step in order to transition to the gospel.

Be wise in the way you act toward outsiders; make the most of every opportunity. *Let your conversation be always full of grace*, seasoned with salt, so that you may know how to answer everyone. (Colossians 4:5–6)

Build Genuine Relationships

From these verses, you can see that God expects even the most tongue-tied Christian to interact with outsiders in conversation. If God is going to open doors in conversation, it will happen as we build genuine relationships with unbelievers. The gospel message travels best from one person to another over the bridge of a genuine relationship. In this chapter, we will consider what genuine relationships are and where we build them. In the next chapter, we will examine how to be wise in building those genuine relationships.

Not a Phony Relationship

What exactly is a genuine relationship? Let's start by examining what a genuine relationship is not. A genuine relationship is *not a phony relationship*. To be genuine is to be real, sincere, and honest. A genuine relationship occurs when we are being sincere in our conversation, not fake or artificial. We stop being genuine when, in our own strength, we try to turn a conversation to spiritual things. Much like a used-car salesman, we might not be really interested in the other person. Our only interest is in making the "sale;" that is, turning the conversation to the gospel. Any friendly, preliminary conversation is only to help us make a faster "sale."

Slowly, I realized God is the only one who can open doors for the message to be shared. I cannot. When I tried to force open a door, I failed. When he opened the way, the conversation was Spirit-led and natural. Realizing that God had to create the opening, I began to relax and interact with people more sincerely. Now I talked with them as individuals made in the image of God. I did not try to manipulate the conversation toward spiritual things. If God opened a door for the gospel, then I was ready. If God did not open a door, I was not going to force one open. As a result, I began to relate to people genuinely, without hypocrisy.

Any evangelistic method that encourages us to manipulate the conversation is not helpful. It will bother our conscience and cause us to feel dishonest. Instead of being genuinely interested in a person, we are acting. And play-acting is the definition of hypocrisy.

As bearers of the message of eternal life, our job is to genuinely love the people we meet. Rather than feel pressured to turn the conversation to spiritual things, we are to pray and ask God to open a door. As we sincerely interact with non-Christians, they will feel our love and sincerity. And if God opens a way for the message, they will not feel manipulated.

Not Necessarily a Friendship

If we can err on the side of being too shallow and uninterested in a person before we share the gospel, we can also err on the other side. A genuine relationship that serves as a bridge for the gospel is *not necessarily a friendship*. Many recent books have encouraged us to befriend non-Christians in the hope of sharing our faith. These books rightly pull us into the non-Christian's world. But in my own life, there were two unintended consequences of trying to befriend non-Christians.

First, I wrongly assumed that I could not talk with a person about spiritual things unless I had invested heavily in that relationship. Actually, this assumption caused me to share less. None of us has enough time to befriend all the non-Christians we could. Friendships take time, and life is busy. In addition to the biblical call to evangelize, there are commands to love our families, love the church of Jesus Christ, use our spiritual gifts, study the Bible, and so forth. Add in the demands of work, extended family, maintaining a home, and guess who is squeezed out? The lost. If I will only share the gospel with non-Christian *friends,* then I will probably share my faith once every couple of years. I don't think that is God's plan for his children.

My second wrong assumption was that my friendship would be enough to win my friend to Christ. I thought if I could only show him the love of Christ and the peace in my heart, then he or she would be attracted to Jesus. The truth is that some people will not be won over to the gospel no matter how much you befriend them. They may enjoy the benefits of your friendship much as the crowd enjoyed Jesus' provision of bread. But the crowd was not interested in the bread of life (John 6:25–42). In my life, friendship evangelism became a lot of friendship and very little evangelism.

A Genuine Relationship

It is more realistic to accept that there are different kinds of genuine relationships. A genuine relationship may include a friendship, but a friendship is not a prerequisite to sharing your faith. When Jesus talked with the Samaritan woman, she was not a friend of his. They had just met. Yet Jesus built a genuine relationship with her and then shared the good news about himself (John 4:1–26). Philip interacted with the Ethiopian eunuch in a similar manner (Acts 8:26–40). In both cases, they had just met the people with whom they shared the good news.

As you seek to build genuine relationships with unbelievers, you will realize that those relationships come in many forms. There is the genuine relationship you have with your co-workers, which is different from the genuine relationship you have with the person who cuts your hair. That relationship in turn is different from the relationship you have with the parent you just met on the playground.

If we treat people genuinely and wait for God to open the doors, we can share the gospel in all types of relationships. For example, the Lord opened the door for me to share with several of my co-workers who were not close friends. Several other times I have had the opportunity to share with people I met once and never saw again. Although these people were not friends, in each of those situations I was relating to them genuinely and waiting to see if God opened a door. When he did open the door, I was able to walk through it.

Where Do I Build Genuine Relationships?

Before we talk about how to build genuine relationships, we need to ask, "Where do we build those relationships?" The best answer to the question is, *As we go.*

When we look at Jesus' Great Commission to his disciples in Matthew 28:18–20, we see that the two prominent commands are (1) go and (2) make disciples. Based on this and other verses, we rightly conclude that the Church of Christ is to take initiative in reaching out. We do this in many ways, including sending out missionaries, conducting formal evangelistic campaigns, and sponsoring official church visitation teams. These are excellent answers and certainly are a fulfillment of this command.

But if we are not one to officially go, like as a missionary or even on a church visitation team, then it is easy for the tongue-tied Christian to put this command out of his or her mind. After all, we say to ourselves, we cannot evangelize all the time. We have to go to work. We have to take care of our families. We have other ministries in the church to do. And so we make an unbiblical distinction between evangelistic people, like a missionary or pastor, and non-evangelistic people, like the rest of us.

But the main command of this passage is "make disciples." So even in times when we are not officially "going," Jesus' followers are still called to make disciples. While certainly Christians are to go, we must not overlook the opportunities we have as we go about our everyday activities.

As You Go

So where are you to build genuine relationships? Build genuine relationships as you go about your day. As you go for your haircut. As you go to your high school or college class. As you go to your dog show. As you go to your craft class. As you go to work. As you go to the playground. As you go to your high school reunion. As you go (and wait!) for your child at soccer. As you go to the dentist. As you go on a business trip. As you go to pick up the pizza. As you go on a sales call. *As you go.*

By realizing that we are to make disciples as we go, life becomes a treasure hunt. We begin to look for doors that God is going to open. Paul writes that God:

> determined the times set for [men] and *the exact places* where they should live. God did this so that men would seek him and reach out for him and find him, though he is not far from each one of us. (Acts 17:26–27)

Perhaps one reason you are at this job or taking this class or at this playground is so that you will have contact with the others who are there. Since God controls everything, he has ordained that *all of those people* be there.

Before we had children, my wife worked in a stockbroker's office for one year. She would often witness to a broker there who seemed friendly yet antagonistic to the gospel. Eventually, we developed enough of a relationship with him that we became acquainted with his wife. Sue trusted Christ first. John came to the Lord several years later. And now they have since led several others to Christ. Why was Sharon at this job? One reason was to come into contact with this family.

As You Go to Work

One of the most natural places to build genuine relationships is at work. Work is where we go most often. Many of us spend eight or more hours with our co-workers everyday. They know our character and the quality of our work. Alan Wolfe, in his *One Nation, After All,* makes this observation:

> It is the workplace where most people learn about themselves, find out which values are truly important, make friends, develop their networks, eat their lunch, give to charity, fall in love, discuss television and sports, and learn what's on the minds of other people.[7]

Most of us are closer to our co-workers than the neighbors on our street. As a result, the gospel travels well at work. In our church, over half of the men who became Christians as adults came to Christ through the witness of a co-worker.

God has always spread his message in places of commerce. For example, the land God gave to his people was at the center of the ancient trade routes between Egypt, Babylon, and Asia. In the normal rhythm of commerce, foreign traders would travel through and naturally come into contact with the God of Israel. They, in turn, would bring this knowledge back to their people. Today, God still uses business relationships as a normal method of spreading the gospel.

Yet the work environment is one of the most secular environments around. Sports, weather, and family are acceptable topics of conversation. Grumbling about the boss and other workers is acceptable. But talking about religion is not. If we are going to bring the gospel to our co-workers, we need to learn how to transition through the secular barriers to the gospel. We will discuss this point in chapter 5.

If you work outside the home, realize that God often uses business relationships as a bridge for the gospel. Whether employer or employee, you are in full-time Christian work. Your mission field is the people you come in contact with at work. Look for opportunities to sow the word among them.

As You Go through Trials

In addition, we can also build genuine relationships as we go through trials. Our trials can actually serve to further the gospel. Jesus promised his disciples that they would receive persecution. "And you will be brought before governors and kings for my sake, as a testimony to them and to the Gentiles" (Matthew 10:18). What the disciples might have viewed as random persecution and defeat for the gospel was actually part of God's plan to reach the government officials!

Paul understood this truth when he wrote from jail, "Now I want you to know that what has happened to me has really served to advance the gospel" (Philippians 1:12). He viewed his circumstances in light of the progress of the gospel. Far from being discouraged by sitting in a Roman jail, he was rejoicing. The message of the gospel was progressing because of his suffering.

In a similar way, God often derails our plans with trials. But in God's sovereignty, those very trials can actually serve to advance the gospel. Some trials are large. But God can still use those to spread the message. A good friend wrote this about his father-in-law's struggle with terminal brain cancer:

> Last Friday, Don was released from Yale-New Haven to go to the Chestelm Nursing Home in East Haddam, Connecticut. During this sixty-five-day "visit" at Yale-New Haven Hospital, Jesse, a personal care attendant in the neurological unit, came to faith in Christ. Her co-workers said she'd find help for her problems with "those people in that room—they always pray a lot."

This story illustrates building genuine relationships as you go through trials—even in the hospital!

But God is also at work in small trials. For example, although we had lived in our neighborhood for eight years, we barely knew any neighbors beyond those immediately surrounding us. All that changed when a neighbor informed us that our tiny street was to be turned into a through road. With a common enemy, the neighborhood rallied together. A neighborhood association was formed, and I was one of three members elected to a steering committee. Out of this unexpected problem came closer neighborhood relationships and several chances for me to spread the message. (And, yes, we stopped the road from coming through.)

God will place similar situations in your life. You can fight with God, or you can see these problems as a chance to share the gospel. As we embrace these trials, our attitude should be like that of Joseph toward his brothers. "You intended to harm me, but God intended it for good to accomplish what is now being done, the saving of many lives" (Genesis 50:20). What you think of as harming you can in fact serve to advance the gospel.

Go into the World

After a little reflection, some Christians may realize that they don't have any significant contacts with unbelievers. They are unable to obey the command to act wisely toward outsiders because they only interact with insiders. All their friends are Christians. They fill their week with Christian Bible studies and phone conversations with fellow believers. Retirees, homemakers, and pastors are particularly vulnerable to this trap. What is the answer for the Christian already pressed for time? *While doing something else* develop relationships with non-Christians.

Have you wanted to learn more about personal computers? Take a class for the purpose of learning about personal computers *and* developing relationships with unbelievers. Do you need to exercise more? Join a gym for the purpose of exercise *and* developing relationships with unbelievers. Leave the Christian "ghetto" and become acquainted with non-Christians in your area.

God expects that his children will interact with outsiders as we go throughout life. As we treat people genuinely, without hypocrisy, God will open doors for the message to go forward. We can relish looking for these divine openings in each day.

For Thought, Discussion, and Action

- After taking a class on sharing your faith, have you ever felt you were being asked to build a phony relationship with another person? Why? Did it bother your conscience? How did you respond?

- Have you fallen into the trap of believing you can only share your faith with friends? What have been some positive results of this belief? What are some negative results of this belief?

- Where do you typically go during a week? Where can you initiate conversations and build genuine relationships with unbelievers as you go about your life?

- How effective have you been in bringing the gospel to those with whom you work? What new insight does this chapter give you?

- Can you look back on any trials and see how they might have been used to advance the gospel through the new relationships God brought into your life?

- Do you fit in the category of those who have few significant contacts with unbelievers? What could you do with a secondary purpose of rubbing shoulders with unbelievers?

CHAPTER 4

Acting Wisely and Speaking Graciously

How do tongue-tied people build genuine relationships? Again, God gives us the answer in Colossians 4:5–6.

Be wise in the way you act toward outsiders; make the most of every opportunity. *Let your conversation be always full of grace*, seasoned with salt, so that you may know how to answer everyone.

Notice that it is only as we act wisely and speak graciously that we will know how to answer everyone. Each person we talk to will be at a different place in his or her spiritual pilgrimage. If we don't act wisely and speak graciously, we may *speak at* them, but we will not be able to *answer* them.

Take the Initiative

The first way to treat people wisely is to *take the initiative* in the relationship. Jesus clearly modeled this pattern for us. "When a Samaritan woman came to draw water, Jesus said to her, 'Will you give me a drink?'" (John 4:7). Notice that Jesus initiated the relationship. In doing so, he overcame three barriers: Jews did not talk to Samaritans; men did not talk to women; and rabbis did not talk to sinners. Jesus, however, ignored all of these barriers and took the initiative.

In the Sermon on the Mount, Jesus taught, "If you love those who love you, what reward will you get? Are not even the tax collectors doing that? And if you greet only your brothers, what are you doing more than others? Don't even pagans do that?" (Matthew 5:46–47). Here, Jesus observed that by greeting only fellow Christians, we are showing no more love than the world shows. The obvious application is that Christians ought to greet all people. Greeting another person is one of the most basic expressions of love there is.

Take the Initiative with Questions

In the reserved parts of the country, like the Northeast, any initial conversation must usually start with the believer. Whether on the airplane or on the playground, people generally don't initiate conversation. Often just a few simple questions will start a conversation.

Such questions must be appropriate to the situation. For example, on the playground, parents will often ask, "How old is your child?" "What is his name?" "Do you come here often?" and similar questions. On the airplane the appropriate questions are "Where are you heading?" and "Business or pleasure?" In a situation where it might be appropriate to start a conversation but I cannot think of a question, I will ask the Holy Spirit, and one always comes to mind. Those of us who are severely tongue-tied might benefit from thinking through a few questions ahead of time.

Take the Initiative by Seeking Them

More foundational in taking the initiative is having a willingness to seek out non-Christians. Our own hearts must be willing to overcome our fear and protectiveness, so that we are willing to seek out lost people. Jesus said he came "*to seek* and to save what was lost" (Luke 19:10). The good shepherd leaves the ninety-nine sheep and goes out looking for the lost one (Luke 15:4). When we seek after lost people, we are actually imitating God. Will you seek them? Given a choice between talking with a fellow believer and befriending a non-Christian while waiting for your child's soccer practice to end, which would you choose? Though it is natural to be drawn to the

Christian, which one is in danger of an eternity apart from God? Perhaps God has put you in this situation so that this person will hear the gospel. But you must seek them.

Be prepared and willing to take the initiative to start conversations with unbelievers. Love them enough to overcome the shyness you may feel. Ask and remember their names. Prepare simple questions, and rely on the Holy Spirit to aid you in this endeavor.

Accept People as They Are

A second way to treat people wisely is to *accept them as they are.* Many Christians are surprised when they begin to talk to a non-Christian that he or she acts so . . . (gasp!) . . . sinful. Jesus was a friend of sinners. He reserved his judgment for the Pharisees. He expected the sinner to act like—a sinner! Rather than being surprised at how sinful some unregenerate people can be, we need to be pleasantly surprised when they have any morals at all. Someone has said that God accepts us the way we are, but he loves us too much to let us stay that way. We must display a similar attitude toward unbelievers.

God tells us that "a friend loves at all times" (Proverbs 17:17). Part of dealing with others wisely is loving them at all times. Paul Little approvingly tells us:

> In his book, *Taking Men Alive,* Charles Trumbell asserts that we can discover in any person at least one thing worthy of an honest compliment. To prove his point, he describes one of his own experiences on a train. A cursing, drunken man staggered into his car. After lurching into the seat beside Mr. Trumbell, he offered him a swallow from his flask. Mr. Trumbell inwardly recoiled from the man. But instead of blasting the man about his condition he replied, "No thank you, but I can see that you are a very generous man." The man's eyes lit up despite his drunken stupor, and the two men began to talk. That day the man heard Christ's claims. He was deeply touched, and later came to the Savior.[8]

Gracious speech like this will communicate love and acceptance to non-Christian people. No matter how sinful, no one is beyond God's love. No one is beyond hope.

Ask Good Questions

A third way to treat people wisely is to *ask good questions*. "The purposes of a man's heart are deep waters but a man of understanding draws him out" (Proverbs 20:5). Good questions communicate interest in the person and help start a conversation. They also allow other people to talk about their favorite subject—themselves. Good questions not only start the relationship but also help deepen it. If used without manipulation, good questions can actually steer the conversation to a certain topic.

It is unfortunate at how inept we Christians can be at developing a relationship by asking questions. Like everyone else, we are in a hurry to talk about ourselves. But the verse above says that if we are persons of understanding and wisdom, we will draw the other person out. Isn't that part of gracious conversation? Besides communicating love and acceptance, we show love by being genuinely interested in the other person and asking skilled questions.

A wise Christian will become adept at asking different types of questions. Learn to ask good questions using the acronym FORC. Ask different questions about the other person's *family* (spouse, children, or grandchildren), *occupation* (What do you do for work? What is your major in college?), *recreation* (What do you do to relax?), or what the two of you have in *common* (for example, how long have you known the hosts of this party you both were invited to). For each subject, ask introductory questions and secondary questions. Introductory questions start a conversation. Secondary questions deepen the conversation and the relationship by asking for more information in some area.

If you really care about speaking graciously, take a little time to think of questions and topics of conversation that will show that you are interested in others. In addition to being prepared, make sure you are asking the questions out of a genuine desire to know the other person and not merely to steer the conversation to the gospel.

Be Quick to Listen

A fourth element in acting wisely and speaking graciously is to *listen carefully*. "He who answers before listening—that is his folly and his shame" (Proverbs 18:13). In James, the wisdom book of the New Testament, the same principle is stated. "Everyone should be quick to listen, slow to speak" (James 1:19). God also tells us that "a man of knowledge uses words with restraint" (Proverbs 17:27).

Closely connected with asking good questions is listening to the answers. We must be genuinely interested in people and their answers. Asking questions is pointless if we don't listen. Could this be why some unbelievers have been offended? Is it possible they are offended not by the message but by the method? Our text says, "Let your conversation be full of grace, seasoned with salt, *so that you may know how to answer everyone*" (Colossians 4:6). But in a typical conversation, we answer before we listen; in fact, we give them the answer before we know the question. Perhaps they understand better than we do that this practice is our folly and shame. Someone has said, "People don't care how much you know until they know how much you care." One way we communicate care is by asking good questions and by listening. We must be genuinely interested in the people and what they have to say.

A friend recently hosted an evangelistic Christmas outreach in her home. The purpose was for Christians and non-Christians to interact, to enjoy the festivities of the season, and at some point, to discuss the reason for the season. But during the mixing time, a Christian guest completely dominated the conversations with the non-Christians. Instead of conversing with them, she talked *at* them. She is funny and endearing, so there was no visible offense. But by not drawing out the other ladies, she ended the night not knowing their hearts. Though she mentioned God, she had no spiritual conversations. These unbelieving ladies went home having listened to a Christian but not having connected with a Christian.

"Where words are many, sin is not absent" (Proverbs 10:19). Many believers need to learn to express love by asking good questions of others, by listening carefully, and by refraining from talking about themselves.

Gifts

A fifth element in acting wisely toward others is to *understand the power of gifts.* "A gift opens the way for the giver" (Proverbs 18:16). One way of expressing love and building relationships is through the giving of various types of gifts. My wife excels at this expression of love. Our elderly neighbors were civil but reserved—until, that is, we invited them over for ice cream one Sunday afternoon. Suddenly the reserve began to melt. What did it cost us? A little ice cream and a little time.

The giving of gifts as a means of opening the way for the gospel is the theme of *Conspiracy of Kindness*. In this book, author Steve Sjogren describes how his and other churches practice acts of kindness as a means of blessing the unsaved. As an expression of God's love, gifts such as free car washes and free soft drinks are given to unbelievers with no strings attached. These gifts often open a relationship with the recipient because they demonstrate Christ's love in a practical manner. Once unbelievers have seen a token of love, they are more ready to hear of God's love in Christ.

How Far Would You Go?

Our church building needed a new roof. On the recommendation of a member, we hired a commercial roofer who specialized in flat roofs. We were told he was "a real stickler for detail." After the work was done by his crew, he came by on a Saturday to inspect. I was in the church building, and we began a conversation about roofing. Excitedly, he wanted to show off his work. Would I climb the three-story ladder to inspect? How far would I go to build a genuine relationship?

I did climb the ladder, and I nodded approvingly as he showed off his handiwork. (Really, though, what did I know about roofing?) Later, after we came down, we continued our conversation. I asked about his business and his family. Then I asked him one of the transition questions we will discuss in the next chapter. The next thing I knew I was handing him a gospel booklet. "Here. Read this," I said, meaning that he should read it later. Instead, thinking I meant that he should read it right then, he began to read it aloud. When we came to the end, he bowed his head and received Christ. What was the cost to me? Climbing a three-story ladder and asking a few questions.

The gospel message will best cross the bridge of a genuine relationship. That genuine relationship may be with a new acquaintance or an old friend. These relationships are built every day through a combination of wisdom and graciousness, qualities the Lord can deepen in us.

For Thought, Discussion, and Action

- How easily do you take the initiative in relationships? Do you wait for others to begin a conversation? Why?
- Is your heart drawn to lost people? Read Luke 15 to gain insight into God's seeking heart. Are there any situations in your life where you have a choice between talking with believers or with unbelievers? Which do you choose? Why?
- Do you have trouble accepting the sinfulness of non-Christians? Are there any sins that you cannot seem to overcome in accepting non-Christians?
- How skilled are you at asking questions of others? Do you know how to become better acquainted through questions? How often do you ask follow-up questions?
- How skilled are you at listening? Do you listen to the answers of others, or are you just waiting for your time to speak? As an exercise, try to have a conversation with someone in your small group or Sunday school class by just asking questions. See how long you can avoid talking about yourself and using the word *I*.
- How do little kindnesses open up a relationship? Can you think of a relationship where an appropriate gift has opened the way for you in the past? Where it might open the way for you (and eventually the gospel) in the future?

CHAPTER 5

Transitioning to the Gospel

S o far we've talked about how to pray for God to open the door and how to build relationships with non-Christians. For a few people, those two steps may be the most difficult to learn. But for tongue-tied Christians, the most difficult part of witnessing is actually bringing up the gospel. We work with people day after day, year after year. We talk about work projects, our families, and our hobbies, but somehow we can never turn the conversation to Jesus.

Even if we could turn the conversation to Jesus, what would we say? We might try to bowl them over with the whole gospel, and they might never talk to us again. Or worse, we would stumble all over our words and look like fools. And the only thing more difficult than being disliked is being laughed at.

You *Can* Share the Gospel

It is easy to deceive ourselves into believing that we cannot share the gospel. Instead, we decide to live upright lives and hope that unbelievers will notice and start asking questions. There are only two problems with that strategy: it is not biblical, and because it is not biblical, it does not work. Over and over Scripture tells us to use words and especially the Word of God.

He chose to give us birth *through the word of truth.* (James 1:18)

For you have been born again, not of perishable seed, but of imperishable, *through the living and enduring word of God.* (1 Peter 1:23)

Everyone who calls on the name of the Lord will be saved. How, then, can they call on the one they have not believed in? And how can they believe in the one of whom they have not *heard*? And how can they *hear* without someone *preaching* to them? And how can they preach unless they are sent? As it is written, 'How beautiful are the feet of those who bring good news!' But not all the Israelites accepted the good news. For Isaiah says, 'Lord, who has believed our message?' *Consequently, faith comes from hearing the message, and the message is heard through the word of Christ.* (Romans 10:13–18)

Salvation comes when someone calls on the name of the Lord. They call after they believe. They believe after they have heard. They hear after someone speaks to them. Verse 17 sums it up beautifully: Faith comes from *hearing* the message.

Once I, a tongue-tied Christian, realize that I must declare my faith verbally, I am immediately confronted with the question of how. Scripture gives us an answer in the text we have been examining.

Be wise in the way you act toward outsiders; *make the most of every opportunity.* Let your conversation be always full of grace, *seasoned with salt* so that you may know how to answer everyone. (Colossians 4:5–6)

In the last two chapters, we considered how to act wisely and speak graciously. In this chapter, we will look at how to make the most of God-given opportunities.

Only God Gives the Opportunities

One key in transitioning to the gospel is to realize that you cannot create an open door. Only God can. Your job is to look for the doors that God is opening and to walk through them. This important principle was presented in chapter 2, but it bears repeating here. Our job is to pray for opportunities. God's job is to make an opening. Once he has, we are to walk through that door.

What a relief! Once we understand this process, a weight of frustration will slide off our shoulders. Now our desire to evangelize can be transformed from drudgery and guilt into an adventure. God will open doors of opportunity for us. Our job is to find those openings hidden throughout our week. If God does not make a way, we haven't failed. We just continue going about our day, praying for open doors, participating in conversations with unbelievers, and trusting that God will work.

Levels of Conversation

Exactly how do we recognize a door that God is opening? Before answering that question, we need to think more deeply about the nature of human conversation. Just a little reflection makes us aware that communication can occur at several different levels.[9]

The first level of communication can be described as *cliché*. People conversing at this level greet each other and mention something shallow. Perhaps they talk about the weather or ask how the other is, but there is no personal sharing. A second level of communication involves the exchange of *information*. While talking at this level we exchange facts about our families, a work project, and so forth. Although the sharing is deeper, it is still not very personal.

The third level involves communicating our *opinions*. Now we are not only exchanging information, but we are also expressing our opinions about it. This is a deeper level of sharing, because we open ourselves to rejection. A fourth level of conversation involves revealing *feelings*. Communication at this level is more vulnerable as we openly share our emotions. Finally, a fifth level of conversation involves *transparency*. Now we are sharing who we really are. At this core level, a person begins to reveal deeply held life beliefs and reasons for them.

Conversation with co-workers, fellow students, and neighbors functions almost completely at the first three levels: cliché, information, and opinions. Talking with others about their beliefs and their spiritual thoughts is several layers down. Those deeper levels involve greater degrees of trust and transparency. Unbelievers can become offended if we try to go too deeply without their permission. However, it is possible, if we ask the right questions, to obtain their permission and then venture into those deeper levels.

Transition Questions

Now that we understand the levels at which conversation can operate and how only God can open a door, how do we talk about spiritual things? The answer is by using a *transition question*. A transition question is a prepared question that takes advantage of a door God opens to turn the conversation to spiritual things.

First, it is a *prepared question*. Doctors, lawyers, reporters, and counselors all are trained to use prepared questions. As a result, they are able to discover important information quickly and skillfully. In a similar way, by having just a few thoughtful questions prepared and memorized, even the most tongue-tied Christian can open the door to deeper levels of conversation.

Second, it takes advantage of a door *God opens*. Again, it cannot be overemphasized that God is the one who has to open the door. If you think you can open it, you will fail. But if you are praying, you will be relaxed and watching for God to work. And when God opens a door, we need to be ready to take advantage of it. A transition question will help you walk though the open door.

Third, a transition question turns the conversation to *spiritual things*. Rather than immediately talking about Jesus, you begin progressing through the conversation levels by talking about spiritual things in general. Interestingly enough, once people give you permission to talk on this level, you can usually speak about spiritual things a second time without God having to specifically open the door again.

"Are You Interested in Spiritual Things?"

By far, the most important transition questions you can learn are these: *Are you interested in spiritual things?* and *What are your spiritual beliefs?* These questions succeed for several reasons. First, you are asking their opinion. It shows that you are interested in their thoughts and beliefs. You are showing respect for them. A conversation involves give-and-take between two people. Christians trying to share their faith often do too much talking and too little listening. When we speak before listening, it is our folly and shame (Proverbs 18:13). Gracious speech includes a genuine interest in unbelievers and in their thoughts.

The second reason that these are such powerful questions is that they can move the conversation down a level in a non-threatening way. The conversation has transitioned to a deeper, more personal level. We are not talking about their church background, which can leave the conversation shallow. Nor are we talking about Jesus yet. We are at a safe place—their interest in spiritual things. These questions allow them to define spiritual things however they want.

Why ask the question? Your goal in asking your friends or acquaintances about their spiritual beliefs is to draw them out. By asking questions, you are communicating interest and respect. But even more importantly, you are trying to understand them. The result of acting wisely and speaking graciously is "so that you may know how to answer everyone" (Colossians 4:6). By listening and probing with questions, we can actually know how to answer each person we talk with.

Having said this, we need to realize that most people think little about their beliefs. Every time you hear a teaching in your church or Bible study, you are adding to your own understanding. In contrast, most unbelievers invest very little time thinking about their beliefs. Their opinions are usually a patchwork of ideas they have picked up through life. So inquire about those beliefs, but don't expect them to be very articulate. When appropriate, turn the conversation to Jesus.

One well-meaning friend attempted to put these principles into effect but spent too much time asking questions. Instead of using the question to transition to the gospel, he felt he first must probe the depths of his new friend's beliefs. He needed to realize that after just a few questions, he had probed the extent of his friend's understanding. It was then time to move on to proclamation.

Religion: The Door to Deeper Conversations

If you have been praying that God will open a door for your message, and if you have been acting wisely toward outsiders, then God is going to open an opportunity. The key is to recognize the door and to be ready for it.

The most common opportunity that the Lord can give in conversation is the topic of religion. It is easy to move from talking about religious things to asking your transition question. Religion can come up as you discuss your church involvement, their church involvement, the news, and many other common topics. Anything religious that comes up in conversation can lead into your transition question.

While many people are uneasy about talking about their beliefs, often they are quite comfortable talking about religion or church. They might be involved in a church, even though they are not born again. Even if they aren't involved, they probably respect your involvement. Most people have reasonably positive feelings about "organized religion." As a result, the subject of religion will come up quite naturally. But most unbelievers also see religion as irrelevant to them and their daily living. Just remember, when you are talking about church involvement, you are still talking at the information level. You are not talking about their beliefs down at the level of transparency.

In addition, many people are becoming more interested in talking about "spiritual things." Even among those who have no use for church, there has been a renewed interest in spirituality. Materialism has left our country feeling empty inside, and many who would never darken the door of a church building have developed some interest in their spiritual lives. Spirituality has made a comeback and can be talked about quite naturally.

We know that ultimately our goal is not to talk about religion or spirituality but to talk about Jesus, our Savior. But arriving at that point in everyday conversation is difficult. To bring up the subject of Jesus, we often have to walk down the path of spirituality and let them tell us about their spiritual beliefs.

Frank and Doug

Frank had worked beside my cubicle for several years. We had a great relationship and had talked about everything: our work, our families, and our hobbies. He knew I was "religious," but I never had talked to him about the Lord. I knew he was Catholic in name only. His Sunday mornings were usually spent camping with his family. As I discovered these principles of evangelism, I began praying that God would open a door for the message.

One day out of the blue, he said to me, "This Episcopal church next to my house has a new sign that reads, 'Contemporary Worship.' For us Catholics, anybody else's worship service has to be contemporary." And he laughed.

We talked about what the sign meant, and then I said to him, "You know we've worked together for a while, but I've never asked you about your beliefs. Are you interested in spiritual things?"

For the next fifteen minutes we talked about what he believed and didn't believe and what I believed. God had opened a door for the message. I had not forced it open. Frank had brought up the topic of religion. We talked about the topic for a little while, and then I was able to move the conversation to a deeper level with my prepared transition question. God had opened the door, and I was prepared to walk through it.

Similarly, Doug and I had been working together for several years. One day he asked me for a ride to pick up his car. As we drove the short distance, we had this conversation.

"Chap, what are you doing this weekend?"

"I'm a part-time pastor, and I actually work on Saturdays, so that's what I will be doing tomorrow. I've never asked you, do you have any interest in spiritual things?"

"No, I don't believe in a personal God and all that stuff."

"Why not?"

"I remember sitting in catechism class . . ."

He went on for a few more sentences, and then we were at our destination. Before he left the car, I probed a bit further for his interest.

"I'd love to continue this conversation with you."

"Me too," he responded.

"Let's have lunch sometime."

"Sure, how about next week?"

With that conversation, a lunch discussion began that continued once every couple of weeks for six months. In the conversations with both Frank and Doug, the topic of religion had come up quite naturally. At the end of talking about religion, the conversations moved to a deeper level by asking about an interest in spiritual things.

Your Church Activities

Any time religion comes up in a conversation or could come up can be an open door. Often we are asked, "What did you do this weekend?" or "What's new in your life?" In the past, out of fear, I would mumble some answer that had nothing to do with the Lord's work in my life or my church involvement. But then I realized that these questions were natural lead-ins to discuss my religious activity and then transition to spiritual things.

When someone asks you a question and the answer involves church, don't avoid the question. Answer it and then transition to spiritual things. If you went on a church retreat this past weekend, tell them about it. If you were involved in a church play this past weekend, tell them about it. Perhaps you accompanied your children on a youth group outing this past weekend or attended a Bible study group the previous night. Did you have to leave work to go to a church member's funeral? No matter what the activity, be genuine and transparent about your life.

Don't hold back from bringing up your activities out of fear of appearing religious. To a secular world, you are very religious. But at the end of that short description of your activity, use the transition question—"Are you interested in spiritual things?"—to move from religious activity to spiritual things and from your life to theirs.

Other Religious Topics

In addition, other religious topics can prompt your transition question. Perhaps there is something about another person that lets you know they have *an interest in spiritual things*. Maria was a doctor's receptionist. One of the members of our church went for a doctor's appointment and noticed several religious sayings that Maria had on the wall. She asked Maria about them to start the conversation. Eventually she invited Maria to our church. A few weeks later Maria invited Christ into her life. Since then her sister has become a Christian, and others in Maria's family are hearing the gospel—all because one woman transitioned to spiritual things at her doctor's appointment.

A co-worker gave me some *religious jokes* that someone had given her. Since she had brought up the topic of religion, here was an open door to begin talking about spiritual things and her beliefs.

If someone *shares a problem* with you, you could offer to pray for him or her at that moment or in your small group. Such an offer gives you a chance then or later to ask if they have any interest in spiritual things.

Negative religious reports can be an open door. If someone brings up a scandal-ridden ministry that has been exposed in the news, you can agree with them, saying something like, "Isn't it amazing how far people can move from Jesus' teachings?" Then use the transition question to ask about their beliefs.

As you can see from these examples, there really is no limit to the opportunities to transition to the gospel. The key is to shift religious conversations to the next level by asking a transition question. As you pray for God to open a door for the message and build genuine relationships with unbelievers, the subject of religion will arise. If you are prepared and dependent upon the Holy Spirit, you will be able to transition the conversation to a deeper level. And then the fun begins!

Use Common Questions

Another way to recognize open doors is to examine *common questions* you are regularly asked. Think them through and determine whether there is a way to transition to the question about spiritual things.

For example, I moved to Rhode Island to go to college. I ended up staying to be a part of a church-planting movement in that state. Every so often, I will be asked where I am from. When I tell them I grew up in Alabama, invariably the next question is, "How did you end up in Rhode Island?" For a long time, my answer to that question bothered me. I wanted to use my answer to talk about the Lord. Instead, I would end up saying something about going to college up here or starting churches in the area. Their response to that answer? A blank stare, an uncomfortable silence and the change of the conversation back to something less threatening, more related to their life.

Then the Lord taught me these principles. Now I answer their question by giving the story of my convincing (see chapter 6 and appendix B) and then turn the conversation to spiritual things. If someone asks, "How did you end up here in Rhode Island?" I answer something like this: "I came up here to go to college. While here I started asking if there was really any purpose to life, which I guess a lot of college kids do . . ."

And then I launch into a short two-minute testimony. At the end, I transition from religion to spiritual things by asking this question: "So that's how I ended up staying in Rhode Island. What about you? Do you have any interest in spiritual things?"

Other common questions that lead into "religion" can be used to transition to the gospel. For the pastor, the common question "What do you do for a living?" is a natural lead-in to ask the transition question.

The same is true for those who homeschool or send their children to Christian schools. A common question is "Where do your children go to school?" When you answer, also offer an explanation of why you have made this educational choice. Relate it to your spiritual beliefs. At the end of your short explanation, ask if they are interested in spiritual things. Don't focus on the benefits of homeschooling or Christian schools; instead, focus on their need for the Savior. After all, which is more important?

Any common question that leads into religion is an open door to talk about spiritual things. Do you attend a Christian college? When asked where you go to college, give your answer, and then ask about their spiritual beliefs. Did you go on a missions trip this summer? When asked what you did this summer, tell a little about the missions trip and then ask about their interest in spiritual things. Anything can be an open door to talk about spiritual beliefs. Your goal is to engage as many people as possible in talking about their beliefs.

God Will Make a Way

In response to your prayers, God will open doors for you. Amazingly, sometimes those doors will open after talking with people only a few minutes. Our job is to be relaxed and sensitive to the Holy Spirit, looking for open doors. Frequently, the opportunity will occur when the topic of religion comes up in conversation. When it does, ask your prepared transition question with a genuinely interested heart. You will be able to watch in amazement as the conversation drops to deeper levels. Whether with old friend or new acquaintance, you will have an enjoyable conversation about deeply held beliefs. When that happens, give God the glory. He has just opened a door for you, his ordinary messenger, to begin communicating his extraordinary message.

For Thought, Discussion, and Action
- At what level do you talk with your co-workers? Your friends? Your spouse? What causes conversations to move deeper naturally?
- Do you talk freely with unbelievers about your religious activities, or do you downplay them? Why?

- What are some religious conversations you have had in the recent past? How did they start? How did they end? Would they have continued with a transition question?
- What are some common questions you receive that relate to the subject of religion? How could you end with a transition question?
- Pray that God would bring up the topic of religion this week in a conversation, so that you might be able to transition to spiritual things.

CHAPTER 6

Unleashing Your Stories

In the last chapter, you learned how God will open a door for the message through the conversational topic of religion. If we are praying, and if we are prepared, there is another door that God will open as well: stories of how God has worked in your life.

If you are truly tongue-tied, that thought will put fear in your heart. "What stories do I have?" Perhaps you have been hindered in the past because you don't have a powerful conversion story. But if you are a child of God, I am sure that you have many wonderful times of God's work in your life. The problem is that you've never thought about using those stories to share your faith with others. By the end of this chapter you will have several stories that can help you transition to the gospel.

Your Stories Are Powerful

Throughout the Bible, God has used the accounts of ordinary men and women to influence others. Stories are powerful for many reasons. First, *they are personal.* The stories you have are not about some high and holy person, but an average person—you!

Second, *they cannot be argued with.* No one can dispute your experiences. They may dismiss your conclusions as wishful thinking, but they cannot argue with your experience.

Third, *people love stories.* God has made us this way. What are movies, novels, and TV programs? Stories. The Old Testament from Genesis to Nehemiah is historical stories. What method did Jesus use most often to teach? Stories. God has made us to love and remember stories.

Fourth, *they invite hope.* If your story relates to the problems the listener is having, then it will give them hope. When you tell someone about how Jesus has changed your life for the better, they will listen.

Fifth, and most importantly, they are a *biblical method* of spreading the good news. In fact, Jesus commanded the demoniac:

> "Go home to your family and tell them how much the Lord has done for you, and how he has had mercy on you." So the man went away and began to tell in the Decapolis how much Jesus had done for him. And all the people were amazed. (Mark 5:19–20)

After encountering Jesus, the woman at the well did the same.

> Then leaving her water jar, the woman went back to the town and said to the people, "Come see a man who told me everything I ever did. Could this be the Christ?" (John 4:28–29)

Her account was evidently powerful because "many of the Samaritans from that town believed in him because of the woman's testimony" (John 4:39). How much theology did she have right? Very little! But that did not stop her from telling her story to her friends.

In the same way, the beggar who was healed of his blindness told his story to the Pharisees. They wanted to prove Jesus was sinful. The blind man's response? "Whether he is a sinner or not, I don't know. One thing I do know, I was blind but now I see" (John 9:25). Here's the power of a story. Did the man have the answers to all their questions? Of course not. But the simple narration of how Jesus worked in his life confounded and convicted the religious leaders. Personal stories always triumph over theological bickering.

Even with all his theological training, Paul used his conversion story when speaking with his fellow Jews (Acts 22:1–22) and when speaking with King Agrippa (Acts 26:1–23). Your stories can also be that powerful!

Be Ready with an Answer

If you are praying for God to open a door for the message and you are building genuine relationships with people, you will share your stories. Thinking through your stories beforehand is not only wise; it is absolutely essential for the tongue-tied. If we really care about a presentation, we will prepare for it.

Anyone who has ever interviewed for a job prepares for the interview. He or she jots down key points to bring up and thinks through the answers to common questions. Rather than a hindrance, this preparation actually frees us to more fully concentrate on the conversation. Whether being interviewed for a job or for the gospel, preparation is the key. Scripture tells us, "*Always be prepared* to give an answer to everyone who asks you to give the reason for the hope that you have" (1 Peter 3:15).

Thinking through your stories and writing them down will result in maximum benefit. You will be able to concentrate more fully on the other person and the needs of the moment. The discipline of writing your stories down will also keep you from dominating the conversation. The most common mistake in telling others our story is to talk too long and provide details that are not relevant to the listener. When that happens, a conversation turns into a monologue and the listener tunes out. Most training programs recommend limiting your story to three minutes. Is it just a coincidence that, when read aloud, Paul's story (for example, in Acts 26:1–23) also lasts three minutes?

Different Types of Stories You Have

Many evangelistic programs encourage you to develop your "testimony." I have deliberately stayed away from this word. In evangelical lingo, the word *testimony* has come to mean the story of your conversion. This works well for those who had a definite conversion as an adult or teenager. But because I professed Christ as a young child, I don't have an adult conversion story. Does that mean I don't have a story to tell?

The answer to this question is found in thinking more broadly about how God has worked in our lives. There are really three different types of stories you can develop. If you were saved as a teen or adult, then develop the story of how you were *converted*. But if you were saved as a child, you may be able develop the story of how you were *convinced* as a teen or adult. Finally, all of us can develop several stories of how we have *coped* with life's common problems. Let's take a closer look at these three.

The Story of Your Conversion

If you were saved as an older teen or adult, then your first story is about how you came to the Lord. There are a number of good resources available to help you with this story. I have included a worksheet in appendix B. Additional help can be found at the web site www.tonguetied.org. There are three parts to this story: your life before you came to Christ, how you came to Christ, and your life after you came to Christ.

First, write a few sentences describing what your life was like before you received Christ. Specifically, you want to state those symptoms of sin that caused you to begin feeling the need for the Savior. Examples would include guilt, emptiness, and so forth. See appendix B for more examples.

Second, state clearly and simply how you came to Christ, including only the parts of the story relevant to the most listeners. If the process took several years and included many people, you would include only the highlights. Remember who your audience will be. Although your church family may appreciate knowing all the people and the different impact they had on you, the listener will not. It is also important to include a Scripture verse that was meaningful in your coming to Christ.

Third, state the benefits you have received from following Christ. These should probably tie back to the symptoms of sin mentioned at the beginning. Be genuine and don't exaggerate. But do state the positive benefits.

It will take discipline to write out what you are going to say, but you will benefit from the preparation. When you are finished, put your story aside for a few days. Then come back and read it from the perspective of an unbeliever who does not know any Christian terms or people. Is it short enough to fit into a real conversation? Did you use any "Christian" words that will not be understood by a non-Christian?

Show it to a church leader and a friend for their input. Practice it a few times with a friend to see if it is clear and concise. Nothing kills a conversation more than talking about yourself for a long time. You don't need to have it memorized word for word, but you should be able to remember the main points. By writing down your story and practicing it, you are prepared to make the maximum impact with a minimum of words. Appendix B will give you more help.

The Story of Your Convincing

It could be that the story of your conversion is not relevant to another adult. Maybe you are like me. I was saved at a young age. I'm not sure I even know how old I was. I really don't remember what it was like not to follow the Lord. So how can I write a story that relates to an unsaved adult? What am I going to say, "Before I was a Christian, I used to leave my clothes all around the room. After I became a Christian at age eight, the Lord changed me so that I wanted to pick up my clothes"? If you were saved at a young age, your conversion story could be relevant to a child, but it is probably not relevant to another adult. We find it difficult to share our conversion story with an unbelieving adult because it doesn't relate to them.

Although your conversion story may not be relevant to another adult, you have plenty of other stories that are. The first story you might have that is relevant to another adult is the story of your convincing. Many children who grow up in Christian homes are truly and wonderfully saved at a young age. But sometime in their late teen or college years, they begin asking themselves "Do I really believe this?" "Is this really true?" "Am I going to follow the Lord on my own, or am I going to reject Christianity?" During those dark days, they are wrestling with the Lord. Perhaps they are going through a time of rebellion. If this was true of you, then you experienced some of the same isolation and emptiness that non-Christians feel. When you finally came back to the Lord, there must have been a specific reason. Some part of living apart from God was unattractive. Whether emptiness, guilt, or purposelessness, something caused you to return to Christ. In that returning, you can relate to a non-Christian.

Second-Generation Christians

That twofold pattern aptly describes my own experience as well as a number of second-generation Christians with whom I have talked. As children, we made true professions of faith. But later on, in the high school or college years, there was a time when the faith became our own. We were not following because we had to. We were following because we were convinced.

Paul seems to refer to such a process for Timothy, who grew up in a godly home. Timothy had a Jewish mother and grandmother and was raised in the faith. Paul says to Timothy:

> But as for you, continue in what you have *learned* and have *become convinced of*, because you know those from whom you learned it, and how from infancy you have known the holy Scriptures, which are able to make you wise for salvation through faith in Christ Jesus. (2 Timothy 3:14–15)

It seems that Timothy's walk may have had two stages: a time of learning and a time of convincing. If this pattern was true of you, then the story of your convincing will ring true with non-Christians. You can write the story of your convincing just as others might write the story of their conversion. The only difference is that you would not say that you became a Christian. The first section would explain what you were thinking during the time of rebellion or searching. The middle section would explain how your thinking changed. The final section would describe how the Lord has met the needs mentioned in the first section.

The Stories of Your Coping

Maybe you don't have a conversion story that adults will relate to, and perhaps you have always believed and never really needed any convincing. What are you to do? There is a third type of story that everyone has: the coping story.

A coping story is a story of how God helped you handle times of trial and testing. Many of the Old Testament stories that we love are stories of how God helped his people cope with problems.

All around us people are trying to cope with difficult circumstances. Most non-Christians don't let us know the extent of their problems. They may only drop a hint or two. But if we are aware of the many ways the Lord has helped us, then we can tell of that help to others. Difficult problems might include:

- singleness and loneliness problems
- dating or friendship betrayals
- marital problems
- parenting problems
- losing a child to death
- financial problems
- career problems and decisions
- addiction problems
- severe health problems

Or our difficulty might be living with a friend or family member that has one of these problems.

Times when you have walked through difficulties by relying on the Lord are excellent coping stories. The difference between non-Christians and Christians is not that they have problems and we don't. The difference between Christians and non-Christians is that we have the Lord to walk us through those times and they don't. Paul tells us that God gives us trials, so that we will rely on him more (2 Corinthians 1:8–9). Think through the major trials in your life and how the Lord has walked you through them. How could you describe that time in two or three paragraphs to another person facing a similar circumstance?

Following is one of my coping stories that would be relevant to a new parent facing a stressful situation.

One difficult time in my life was right after we had our fourth child in six years, and I was in the midst of heavy demands at work. Those were very rough times on my wife and me. It came to the point where I didn't know how we were going to make it. But each morning before I left, we would hold hands and pray this verse back to the Lord: "Let us approach the throne of grace with confidence, so that we may receive mercy and find grace to help us in our time of need" (Hebrews 4:16). We felt very needy during that time. Every day that we would pray that together, we would make it through the day feeling God's grace. On the days we would not pray, inevitably we would have a bad day.

Take some time before you leave this chapter and list one or two times that were deep valleys for you. Describe it in terms to which a non-Christian could relate. Now think about how you coped with that time better because you were a Christian. How was the Lord more real to you? Write this story down in a few paragraphs so that you could use it in a conversation. The beginning of the story should describe the trial you were facing, followed by a description of how the Lord Jesus was instrumental in helping you through that trial. Remember to be transparent.

Ending Your Stories

When the Lord opens a door for you to bring up one of your stories in a conversation, you still need to know how to end the story. If you don't use the transition question, the ending will be predictable. There will be a moment of awkward silence, and then the other person will change the subject.

To help diminish the awkwardness and to keep the conversation focused on spiritual things, the final sentence of your story is the same: "Are you interested in spiritual things?" This question shows that you are interested in the person who has been listening to you. You are now willing to listen while he or she talks. Remember the whole point in telling your story was to arrive at this point, to transition to spiritual things.

Practical Hints

Keep in mind several points. First, *keep it simple and short*. Me, me, me is dull, dull, dull. Good conversation involves self-revelation. But good conversation also demands consideration. One person (you) cannot dominate the conversation with a ten- (or twenty-) minute story.

Second, *avoid Christian lingo* that makes no sense to your listener. Words like *saved*, *blood of the Lamb*, and *blessed* are words of great value to us who believe, but they don't mean much to the non-Christian.

Third, *create a way to remember the points of your story*. You have worked hard to prepare three or four stories about how the Lord has worked in your life and have fashioned some excellent tools for use in conversation with others. The challenge will be to remember them until you need them. It will be easy to forget them. My suggestion is to write key words for these stories in the front or back of your Bible. That way you will see them on a regular basis. Then you will be ready to tell about how God has been at work in your life. In addition, you will have reminders of how God has worked in your life. These memorials will also be an encouragement to you when you are discouraged.

Fourth, *think about the situations or questions that will prompt your story*. Once you have these tools, when will you actually use them? What conversation topic will prompt the story of your conversion, your convincing, or your coping? What common question will lead naturally into your story? As stated in Chapter 4, one way I transition to the story of my convincing is when asked how I ended up in Rhode Island. I introduce this story by explaining that I came up to Rhode Island to go to college. Then I tell the story of my convincing. I finish by telling them that I decided to stay in the area, and then I ask them if they have any interest in spiritual things. The common question "How did you end up in Rhode Island from Alabama?" always prompts the story of my convincing.

Tell Your Stories

You have a story. In fact, you have several. Others need to hear those stories. "Go home," Jesus says to you, "and tell how much the Lord has done for you" (Mark 5:19). It does not matter whether your conversion was as dramatic as the demoniac's. It does not matter how much theology you know. Like the beggar, all you need to be able to say is "One thing I do know, I was blind but now I see." As you pray for God to open a door, he will give you chances to tell your stories. Be ready, and you will be able to transition to spiritual things. And God will be glorified.

For Thought, Discussion, and Action

- Were you converted as an adult? What caused you to come to Christ? How did your life change?
- If you came to Christ as a child, did you have a time when you were questioning your faith or wandering from the Lord? What was your life like then? What convinced you to follow the Lord now?
- What deep valleys have you been through? How has the Lord sustained you during those times? What kinds of people might be helped by your stories?
- If you don't have any stories, what does that tell you about your walk with God?

- Have you been challenged to write out your stories before? Did you? What barriers stopped you?
- Write out at least two stories: one of your conversion or convincing and one of your coping. Keep them short—three or four minutes, tops. Use appendix B.
- Practice reading your stories to a friend or to your pastor. Have them critique what you wrote for its relevance to a non-Christian, for Christian code words, and for length. Keep editing your stories until you and your friends think they are polished.
- Think about what situations will prompt you to use these stories. Write out these prompts.
- Write out a few phrases to remind you of the key points in your stories. Write them somewhere you will see them regularly, like the flyleaf of your Bible.
- Practice with your friends until you are comfortable. Don't try and memorize what you have written word-for-word. Just work on covering the main points.
- Keep praying that the Lord would open a door for the message and would help you declare the gospel clearly and fearlessly.

CHAPTER 7

Gently Provoking Transitions

J esus said he would make us fishers of men. The previous chapters have described a few nets to use in fishing for men and women. But sometimes he bids us to push out in deeper water. Below are a few means tongue-tied Christians can use if we desire to initiate transitioning to the gospel. However, we must remember to use these with graciousness, supernaturally relying on God.

An Offer to Pray

One easy way to begin transitioning a relationship toward spiritual things occurs when we hear of someone hurting. Prayer to the Ruler of the universe is one weapon we all have in our arsenal. This Ruler just happens to be our Father! Anytime we hear of a way that the devil has come "to steal and kill and destroy" (John 10:10), we should offer to pray.

That offer of prayer can come in several different formats, depending on the situation. We can volunteer to pray aloud for the person at that very moment. Or we could offer to pray for the person during our daily time of prayer. In addition, we can ask to share this request with our small group. After hearing of a difficult situation, it is quite natural to respond, "Would you mind if I prayed for you over the next few weeks?" Or you could say, "I meet together weekly with some friends to pray. Would you mind if I brought this to them for prayer?"

This offer for prayer will be well received for several reasons. First, prayer for someone is inoffensive. Most non-Christians will take all the supernatural help they can receive in a time of crisis. Second, it shows that you care for them. If you are willing to bring their problem up and to remember it over time, it shows genuine love and concern. Third, by asking their permission, you are showing them respect as a person made in God's image.

If you do make this offer, you need to pray! Don't make a promise of prayer and not fulfill it. Make the commitment small if that's all you can fulfill. Remember, when you offer to pray, you are putting God's reputation on the line.

Offering to pray for a friend's need will allow you to provoke spiritual conversations because you have a natural follow-up. It is a natural continuation of your love and concern to ask, "How are things going with . . .?" This follow-up will encourage greater conversation and in turn allow you to pray better. In addition, it will also offer a natural time to ask your friend if he or she is interested in spiritual things or to share one of your coping stories.

Greg and a longtime friend of his were discussing her desire to find another job. She was discouraged because she had been unable to find a job in her field and had not worked in almost two years. He told her that God answered prayer and offered to pray for her job search. She excitedly called back the next week to tell of an interview. Again, Greg offered to pray. Finally she told him she had been offered the job. She said she knew it was because God had answered his prayers. Answered prayer will soften unbelievers to think more about the God who answered the prayer. In addition, it allows us to have further spiritual conversations.

Inviting to an Outreach Event

Another way to gently provoke a transition to spiritual things occurs when we invite people to an outreach event. When we are inviting, our focus is on persuading the person to attend the event. If they attend, they will be exposed to the gospel, and we may think that we have done our part. If they don't attend, we will invite them to another event.

In thinking this way, we overlook another God-given opportunity. Just by bringing up the event, you can ask about their interest in spiritual things and start a conversation. After extending the invitation, it is a natural time to ask "Do you have any interest in spiritual things?" or "What are your spiritual beliefs?" They might not ever darken the door of your outreach event. However, your invitation has given you a chance to bring up spiritual things.

For several years, our church sponsored a Christmas concert that celebrated the season in music and food. Unbelieving relatives and friends came to enjoy an event that would kick off the Christmas season. As expected, many who were invited did not attend. It was only in the last few years that I realized the invitation to the outreach event *itself* was an opportunity to have a conversation about spiritual things.

Years before I understood this principle, I invited three men with whom I worked to a six-week Bible study. Two of them accepted, and the third replied gruffly, "No thanks. I'm not into that stuff." At that point, I decided to steer clear of him and never bring the subject up again. He changed companies, and we lost contact with each other. Years later, a friend met the third man who had so roughly turned me down. When he found out she knew me, he said to her, "I really liked Chap. I wish I had kept in touch." When I heard this, it cut to my heart. Because of one harsh answer, I had given up on him. I have since learned that even a negative response can be turned into a conversation about spiritual things and the relationship kept open.

Prompting Questions

God often commanded Israel to erect memorial stones as a witness to his dealings with them. These pillars were to provoke others to ask, "What do these stones mean?" Then the men of Israel would have a chance to explain God's great work in the past. In a similar way, certain items can provoke questions from unbelievers, so that we can explain God's great work in our lives. For example, my brother-in-law named his pleasure boat *Redeemed*. With other boat names like *Dad's Toy* and *Weekend Pleasure*, his boat's name stood out. As a result, he was asked why he named his boat in this way. This unusual name provoked a natural transition to his testimony.

Similarly, I had placed a provocative bumper sticker on my cubicle wall. The bumper sticker simply stated, "He who dies with the most toys wins . . . nothing (Luke 9:25)." This bumper sticker was a deliberate response to a similar bumper sticker that read, "He who dies with the most toys wins." By hanging that bumper sticker, I was challenging the philosophy of the world and providing a chance to transition to the gospel.

Another situation that provoked questions was when I used to memorize Scripture using 3 x 5 cards while exercising at a gym. The employee with whom I was building a relationship eventually asked me, "What are you doing, preparing for a speech?" Since I had anticipated that question, I was prepared to respond to him and transition to spiritual things. I said, "No. Actually I am reviewing Bible verses. Do you have any interest in spiritual things?"

Using Holiday Events

Christmas has taken over December in our country, with Thanksgiving the final pause before the December rush. Even the most secular person cannot help but notice the inherent Christian message of Christmas. The Church can take advantage of this cultural phenomenon by using holiday events to build relationships and transition to spiritual things.

In our church, several individual ladies host evangelistic cookie swaps around the holiday season. This party involves exchanging different holiday cookies in a festive atmosphere. After a time of socializing, the hostess will invite the ladies to hear an appropriate Christmas story or devotional. To deepen the impact, several ladies have also solicited written prayer requests at the end of the night. This event both builds genuine relationships and uses the holiday to transition to spiritual things.

In the past, our small group caroled in our neighborhood. After singing a few songs, we gave the recipient a gift of holiday cookies and an appropriate piece of literature. One year, the piece of literature was an invitation to our home for a New Year's Day gathering. We hosted this event to further build relationships with our neighbors. At that event, one of them remarked to us that a miracle was taking place—two neighbors who had had a twenty-year feud were in the same room. Through this outreach and open house, grace was overcoming sin.

Handing Out Appropriate Literature

Scripture teaches that we should engage unbelievers in conversation. Often we tongue-tied, fearful Christians would like to anonymously leave a piece of literature or send stories along on the Internet rather than actually engage people in conversation. It is easier to leave a tract in a telephone booth than to stick our necks out in conversation. I have sought to counter this thinking by emphasizing the need for discussion. But in the rush to emphasize dialogue, we must not overlook the value of literature. If used appropriately, a pamphlet can help us open up a spiritual conversation.

One such piece of literature our church has used is *A Christmas Digest*, distributed by Campus Crusade for Christ (see appendix A). There are several reasons this booklet is helpful. First, it uses a season when people are more open to spiritual things. Second, it is large enough that it makes an impression as a genuine gift. Yet it is small enough to be read during the busy Christmas season. Third, and most importantly, it is written with the non-Christian in mind.

Remember, the initial purpose may be to give Christian literature to a non-Christian. But the more important purpose is to allow you to transition a conversation to spiritual things. God's primary way of working is through our conversations with others. Do give out the booklet. But don't give it out instead of talking. Give it out with the hope of starting a conversation about spiritual things.

I once gave one of these books to my boss, saying, "Here's a little something to help you focus on the real reason for the season. When you have time, maybe we could have lunch and discuss it." A short while later, we went to lunch and had a very productive conversation. He told me he had come to believe that our life after death is just like our life before birth—nothing. But then he told me that when he first realized this "truth," he became angry at the purposelessness of life. It is interesting that while denying eternity with his head, he affirms it with his anger. God truly has put eternity in men's hearts (Ecclesiastes 3:11).

Later in our conversation, he related a story about driving himself to the emergency room because of chest pains. He said that he realized at that moment, "I don't have a God to call out to." As a result of this comment, we spent the rest of the time talking about the gospel. He took a Bible and promised to read the chapters to which I directed him.

A Pamphlet with Your Story

Another piece of literature that can prompt conversations is a pamphlet with the story of your conversion or convincing. I know of a few people who have used desktop publishing software to produce an attractive pamphlet with their story in it. These personal accounts can be used in many different situations. For example, if you eat out often, engage the waiter or waitress in conversation and leave your personal pamphlet with a generous tip. Include a handwritten note of thanks for the service. Invite them to contact you at your church's number if you can be of any spiritual help. A personal tract is much more powerful than a generic tract because it is about you, a person they just met.

Even organized outreach programs such as handing out tracts on the street or performing acts of kindness as described in *Conspiracy of Kindness* still should have one purpose: to begin spiritual conversations with unbelievers. Can God use that tract that is being handed out? Of course. But most often he uses the person handing out the tract.

If undertaken with tact, there are many ways we can gently provoke unbelievers to talk about spiritual things. The possibilities are limited only by our imagination and the prompting of the Holy Spirit. Ask the Spirit to show you ways that are appropriate for your situation and your personality.

For Thought, Discussion, and Action

- Have unbelievers shared any problems with you? What was your response at that moment? How could an offer to pray have been helpful? Have you seen answered prayer for unbelievers? Did you follow up with a transition question? Pray for an opportunity to offer prayer to a non-Christian.
- Does your church sponsor outreach events? Do you actively invite people? What kind of response do you receive to the invitation? Do you think those who turned you down would have discussed their spiritual beliefs with you?
- How can you use Christmas as a culturally relevant time for outreach?
- Can you envision using a pamphlet to tell your story to others? Who in your church would have the computer expertise to help you make one?

- Which one of these different ideas can you see yourself attempting? What will stop you from putting this idea into action?

CHAPTER 8

Handling Different Responses

Once you are praying for open doors, building genuine relationships with unbelievers, and asking transition questions, the Lord will use you. He will open doors for the message, and you will move easily to spiritual matters. But then what? What types of answers can you expect from unbelievers? And more importantly, how will you respond to their answers?

You must think through their possible responses. It is at this point that tongue-tied evangelists are snagged most easily. In the past, you may have had difficulty bringing up spiritual things. With that problem past, the next difficulty will be bringing the conversation to the gospel.

Don't worry. The responses you receive to your transition question will fall into one of a few very predictable responses. By preparing for these answers, you will be able to overcome your fear. As you respond, continue to actively pray for the Holy Spirit's empowerment (Acts 1:8).

Answer 1: "No, Not Really"

One response you will receive to the question "Are you interested in spiritual things?" will be, "No, not really." Usually people will be more polite and soften their answer a little bit. But the essence of their answer is the same. If you ask the question, "What are your spiritual beliefs?" they will usually tell you a little bit about their spiritual heritage, if they had one. But they will phrase it in the past tense. "I was raised Jewish but . . .," "I went to Catholic schools growing up but . . ." They are usually secular, materialistic people and think religion is a crutch for those who cannot handle life.

Don't be discouraged or intimidated by these answers. These are the best! The atheistic point of view is unnatural to people. There is usually some reason they are not interested in the spiritual realm. After they say, "No, I'm not too interested," just follow up gently and lovingly by asking, "Oh really? Why not?" Then your conversation will be off and running. Most of the time they will readily tell you what their thinking is. Remember that it is gracious speech coming from a loving person that enables us to ask these bold questions.

In chapter five, I mentioned a conversation with Doug that led to a Bible study. That study started when Doug gave me this answer:

"Are you interested in spiritual things?"

"No. I guess I am too cynical to believe in a personal God. I respect people who do believe, though."

"What do you mean by cynical?"

"Well, if there is a God, he got the world going, and then he took off . . ."

A "no" answer is really a good answer and the easiest answer to handle. As religion has less of an influence in our country, this answer will become more prevalent. Just follow up by asking why they are not interested in spiritual things. Another question that you might use to follow up is, "So, if you aren't interested in spiritual things, what are your spiritual beliefs about life and why we are here?" This is a great question because it asks them to positively state what they do believe.

By probing with these questions honestly and by listening for their answers, you show interest and respect for the person. You are also paving the way to offer the gospel as a natural part of the conversation.

Answer 2: "Yes, I'm Catholic" (or Baptist or Lutheran or Some Other Denomination)

This reply is also a common one. But really this response is not truly an answer to your question. Instead, people have told you what type of church they attend. They have not told you whether they are interested or how active they are. And they have only hinted at what they truly believe. They have just thrown a label back at you. At this point, your discussion is still functioning at the level of information, not the level of belief.

This answer is a little more difficult to handle. It is usually best to affirm their involvement but then press them again. Ask a follow-up question that refocuses on some issue of the gospel. After all, they have told you they are a part of a denomination that professes to follow Jesus. It is only natural that they should be familiar with the gospel, right?

The conversation might proceed as follows (notice the follow-up question in italics):

"Are you interested in spiritual things?"

"I'm Catholic."

"That's great. So you do have an interest in spiritual things. *Are you at the place in your spiritual life where you know for sure you are going to heaven?*"

"No, not really."

"Did you know the Bible says that we can know for certain that if we die we will go to heaven?"

"No, I didn't know that."

"I have a little pamphlet here that sums up the message of the Bible and explains how we can know for certain that we are going to heaven. Could I share it with you?"

Don't become sidetracked with praising or condemning a denomination. After you affirm their involvement, focus your attention on the issue of the gospel. Ask a follow-up question that goes to the heart of their beliefs.

There are several questions you can use if you are prepared. One question made popular by the training program, Evangelism Explosion, is "Have you come to the place in your spiritual life where you know for certain that if you died today you would go to heaven?" This is a powerful and personal question.

Campus Crusade trains its workers to use the follow-up question: "Have you heard of the four Spiritual Laws?" Their standard tool for speaking about Jesus is a pamphlet by the same name. After using this question, the natural action is to take the pamphlet out and begin reading through it with a person.

For someone who is active in a church that does not preach the true gospel, you can ask, "What is your church's view of the third chapter of John?" Most likely, they will not know what is contained in that chapter. At this point, you will have an opportunity to open your New Testament and ask them to read it. Be sure to point out that Nicodemus was a very religious man. The obvious application for them is that even a religious person must be born again. After they have read Jesus' words for themselves, it is appropriate to ask them if they have ever been born again.

Don't speak negatively about any denomination. Your job is to speak about Jesus. The only possible exception to this principle might be if you grew up in that denomination before you became a Christian. If you did, it could be appropriate to tell them the story of your conversion. At the end of your story, you could ask permission to tell them the truths that changed your life.

Be prepared to talk with people who are affiliated with a church to some degree but who have never been born from above. Affirm their involvement but then ask them a follow-up question that goes to the heart of the gospel.

Answer 3: "Yes, I'm Mormon" (or Hindu or New Age or Some Other Non-Christian Religion or Belief)

In our increasingly pluralistic country, we will meet people who are actively involved in a non-Christian religion. Our first reaction to someone with this affiliation may be fear. We think we should know all about these other religions and how to refute them. But we don't. Either we have not been trained or we were trained and we have forgotten. So we clam up for fear that our ignorance will be shown.

Instead, we need to relax. Our approach should be similar to our approach with anyone else. We want to continue our inquiry. What are the central tenets of their beliefs? Do they believe in a form of salvation? How do they believe we achieve salvation? Why do they believe that? What led them to believe this way? Have they ever read the Bible? What do they think about Jesus? Usually, they will be more than happy to talk to us; after all, now *they* are evangelizing *us*.

By continuing my inquiry, I can educate myself with what they believe while at the same time build a relationship. Remember, "He who speaks before listening, it is to his folly and shame." As you inquire about their beliefs, actively compare it to what you know the true gospel to be. After an appropriate time, be ready to tell them what you believe.

If they listen, then you have a chance to make Christ clear. If they don't listen, then at least the Lord gave you a chance to sharpen your understanding of the world's deception.

Answer 4: (Hesitantly) "Yes, I am"

Some people may respond positively to your inquiry, but the tone of their voice or their body language lets you know they are uncomfortable discussing the subject. Perhaps your conversation can be overheard by others. Or perhaps the subject of spiritual things touches a painful issue. In many parts of our country, people are suspicious of strangers and will hesitate to talk about personal things. This is especially true if you have just met.

You can respect that hesitancy while still planting a seed. If this is a one-time meeting, you could give them one of your pamphlets, telling them, "Here is a little booklet that explains where I found peace. Read it if you are interested."

Or if you will see the person again, you can relieve the tension by saying, "Maybe we can talk about it in the future." This response respects their obvious fear. But it also gives you a "foot in the door" to bring up the issue later on. Remember, it's not our job to push the issue. God is the one to open the door for the message and to prepare their hearts.

Questions for Anyone

In *Share Jesus without Fear*, William Fay suggests four other questions that can follow your transition question:

- To you, who is Jesus?
- Do you believe in heaven and hell?
- If you died, where would you go?
- If what you are believing is not true, would you want to know?[10]

These questions are powerful. Anyone can use them, and they cut right to the heart of the issue. Be sure to listen to the answers.

Trust the Holy Spirit to Guide

This short chapter is meant to start you thinking about answers you will receive. Every answer will be a variation of one of these four. By thinking through what our answers will be, we will be ready to continue on to the next step in tongue-tied evangelism.

If you are stumped by an answer someone gives, think of a better answer for next time and write it down. Don't be discouraged. Collect your own answers to these questions. Expect to be baffled at times. Many of the answers in this chapter came from someone stumping me. But then I took that conversation to the Lord and asked for insight as to what I should have said. The next time I heard that answer, I was ready with a response. You can do the same. If you don't know what you should have said, ask a leader in your church. They are given to equip you for these works of service (Ephesians 4:12).

Every time you talk with someone it is a victory. They have stopped their busy life and thought about eternity for a minute. That itself is an accomplishment. In addition, you have grown in your ability. If you persevere in learning from each interaction, you will grow more skillful. Evangelism *can* be learned.

For Thought, Discussion, and Action
- Role-play the different possible responses with some friends. How will you respond to each of these four different types of responses?

CHAPTER 9

Using God-Given Resources

S o, you've finally broken through! You began praying for God to open doors and he did. You built genuine relationships as you went about your day, and suddenly the Holy Spirit opened the door for a conversation. Great! What do you do next?

The fourth step for tongue-tied Christians is to use other resources that God has given the body of Christ. When we started, we admitted that we were not gifted evangelists. We just wanted a few chances of our own to share the gospel. If you followed the instructions in the earlier chapters, you will have spiritual conversations.

But having a conversation about spiritual things is not the same as telling another person about Jesus. The name of Jesus has the power of the gospel and the power of controversy. Although it is good to talk about spiritual things, we must make sure the conversation turns to the person of Jesus.

One of the best ways to discuss Jesus is to use a resource God has blessed in the past. You may be able to transition to this resource at the end of the conversation. Or it may happen a few days later. But don't let the conversation grow cold without following up in some way. When God has opened a door to talk about spiritual things, don't be afraid to bring up the subject of Jesus.

Put Many Tools in Your Toolbox

This chapter presents many resources God has blessed in the past and will continue to bless in the future. Think of them as different tools in your evangelistic toolbox. Someone has said that for the man with only a hammer, everything looks like a nail. In other words, if you have only one tool, you will try to use it in every situation. On the other hand, the more tools you have, the greater your effectiveness can be.

Some of these resources are appropriate for one-time conversations. Others are more suitable when there is an opportunity to follow up. Some will work when people are receptive. Others can be used with those who resist further conversation. Think of them as seed thrown on the soil of the heart (Matthew 13:3–23), ready to bear fruit in God's time. Purchase some of the materials listed below and plan to use them generously. Actively seek the Holy Spirit's guidance as to the resource that is appropriate for each situation.

Pamphlets That Explain the Gospel

The first tool that must be considered is a pamphlet that thoroughly explains the gospel. We have been praying to present Christ clearly. One answer to that prayer is having a person read through a pamphlet with us. Popular ones include *The Four Spiritual Laws,* produced by Campus Crusade for Christ; *Steps to Peace with God,* created by the Billy Graham Evangelistic Association; and *The Bridge to Life,* available from the Navigators. You will find links to these resources at www.tonguetied.org.

There are several advantages to using one of these booklets with every type of unbeliever. First, they explain the gospel simply and understandably. The diagrams that are used also help make the gospel clear. Second, these pamphlets are thorough. By using them, we can make sure we are including the important parts of the gospel. Third, when reading through the booklet with another person, the authority of the gospel is outside of us. By showing them this information in a booklet, we become one beggar showing another beggar where to find the bread of God's Word.

Be sure to use the pamphlets to help you explain the gospel when God has already opened the door. Don't use them to force the conversation. After presenting this material at a seminar, I overheard one mom tell her son that he ought to give his high school friends these tracts. He blushed with embarrassment, realizing that this would never work. I agree with him! His mother was trying to use the pamphlets to force an opportunity. Instead, he should be encouraged to begin praying that God would open a door for the message. When God provided an opening, then the pamphlet could be used to help him explain the gospel.

The gospel moves best across the lines of genuine relationships. When we have that genuine relationship and God makes a way for the message, then a pamphlet can help us articulate the gospel clearly.

Using the pamphlets with religious people. There are several ways to transition to reading through a gospel pamphlet. When talking with people from Christian churches, you can ask if they have ever heard of the booklet. Over one hundred million *Four Spiritual Laws* pamphlets have been printed. It is believed to be the most printed piece of literature in the world. This fact, in and of itself, is a conversation opener.

Often you can ask a person from a religious background what they believe Jesus' central teaching to be. Usually people will make reference to the Golden Rule. At that point, you can tell them you have a leaflet that sums up the central message of the Bible. Ask if they would be interested in looking at it with you.

If they are interested and the situation is appropriate, you could suggest reading through the pamphlet together at that moment. Or suggest reading it together at another time. Say something like, "Maybe sometime in the next week we could read through it over lunch."

Or, if you are really fearful and tongue-tied, you could give a booklet to them and encourage them to read it some other time. I learned the need for the help of a pamphlet the hard way. Soon after the talk with Phil, I had a chance to talk with another person, Carl. God miraculously opened a door, and we had a long and enjoyable conversation about his spiritual beliefs. But I did not present Jesus clearly to him. If I had brought out a booklet during our time together, it would have helped to focus our conversation.

Reading through the pamphlet. If appropriate, ask the person to read the pamphlet out loud. After reading the Scripture verses in the pamphlet, ask them what they think each verse means. They may disagree with what the verse says. But your initial purpose is not for acceptance, just understanding. They can argue all they want to about believing or not believing it. Don't worry about that. Instead, concentrate on having them understand.

If you cannot read through a booklet, it may be appropriate to hand it out. Again, you will hand it out as the Lord provides the occasion for building a genuine relationship. I had been praying that God would open a door for the message. On my lunch hour, I went to a department store that was having a slow day. On the way out, I struck up a conversation with the cashier. He had just recently immigrated to the United States from India. Since no one was in line, we began talking. What part of India had he come from? How long had he been here? Where did he live now? Did he like it in the United States? And then without much forethought, I asked, "Are you interested in spiritual things?" He gave me a brief answer. Knowing that my time was short, I said, "I have a pamphlet that explains the message of the Bible. Would you be interested in it?" "Yes," he replied. I handed him the pamphlet from my appointment book, and then I had to go. Another customer had walked up. I had not gone in the store intending to hand out a pamphlet to the cashier. But I had been praying for God to open a door for the message. And he did.

With the distractions of life, we all need help remembering to use a tool like this. Keep it close at hand and visible, both to remind you to use it, and so that it is available when you need it. I put two in my appointment book, so that I have a copy for myself as well as the person with whom I am talking. Men could put them in their shirt pocket, and ladies might want to put them in their purses. As you put them in your pocket, let it be a reminder to pray for God to open a door for the message. On the back of each one, you can write in the name and address of your church. This will allow the person receiving it to contact you for more information. And you will not be handing out your home address indiscriminately.

Remember, we are not the gifted evangelists. Learning to grow in the skill of transitioning to a pamphlet might take many years. Don't feel overwhelmed. Maybe all you can do now is hand it to a person to read later. That's great! That's more than you were doing before. But don't settle for that. Continue to pray that you would grow in skillful use of one of these pamphlets.

Offer to Have a Short Bible Study

Another available tool is a one-to-one Bible study. This option is even better than the pamphlet for several reasons. First, you build a deeper relationship with the other person over the several weeks of your study. Second, you are exposing the person more deeply to the sword of the Spirit, the Word of God. Third, you are available to tutor them and to answer any question they may have.

Knowing Jesus Christ is an excellent three-study booklet that takes the student through Scriptures that explain who Jesus is, his work on the cross, and how to have eternal life. This booklet is the first book in the NavPress Studies in Christian Living series. See www.tonguetied.org to order this booklet. It is excellent for use in a one-to-one or one-to-two situation. Campus Crusade also provides a valuable resource entitled *Who Is This Jesus?* that takes the students through six short lessons on the life of Jesus. This booklet is meant for use with the *Jesus* film, yet it is an excellent study by itself. For larger group studies, *Your Home a Lighthouse* provides guidelines for hosting a monthly home evangelistic Bible study. In the appendix are actual studies from the gospel of John that you could use word-for-word.

When having a study, it is helpful to read from two identical Bibles. Having matching Bibles is important, so that you can refer to your study passage by page number, and so that you have the same translation. Although most people have a Bible somewhere in their house, it is usually old, dusty, and not in a modern translation. Bibles are available for as little as three dollars and New Testaments for as inexpensively as one dollar. For the price of a soft drink, you can put the Word of God in your friend's hand! Ordering links are at www.tonguetied.org or see appendix A.

Your goal: Make Christ clear. Your goal in this or any Bible study is for your friend to understand who Jesus is. Your job is to make sure the mystery of Christ is clear to them. When Philip saw the Ethiopian eunuch reading the Scripture, he asked, "Do you understand what you are reading?" The man replied, "How can I unless someone explains it to me?" (Acts 8:30–31). This man needed someone to explain the Scriptures. Similarly, most non-Christians need someone to explain the gospel to them.

Obviously, we desire that the person who studies the Bible finish like this man, believing and being baptized. However, we need to remember that conversion is the Holy Spirit's job. Our job is to make the mystery of Christ clear.

For six months Chris and Peter and I had worked together. One day, I invited them to a home Bible study our church was sponsoring. My wife and I, who were newlyweds then, even "bribed" these two single men. We invited them to our house for a home-cooked meal before we left for the study. After six weeks, the Bible study came to an end, and neither one had received Christ. I was disappointed but felt I had been faithful in helping them understand the gospel. When they left for other employment, we drifted apart. Two years later, Chris showed up at church one Sunday; he had come because he needed spiritual help and knew where to find it. He received Christ that day. Like seed that was sown, the gospel needed time to bear fruit.

Special Helps for Work

This story of Chris and Peter highlights the special challenge of bringing the gospel to the workplace. Work will always be one of the best places for daily contact with unbelievers. God uses work relationships in a special way. However, explaining the gospel thoroughly does not usually happen during the work time. Your employer is paying you and the person listening to you to work. It is not ethical to talk about the gospel beyond normal conversation. The Lord will not bless it.

Instead, now that you have learned how to transition to the gospel, you also need to think about when and how this person would hear the gospel. For there to be serious consideration, often a person needs privacy and some uninterrupted time. Some work environments, such as an office, have little privacy. If you sense a person might be open, suggest that you have a short three-week Bible study over lunch. Or offer to go through a gospel pamphlet over coffee.

Perhaps the person is not open to further conversation. In that case, you could leave them with one of these other materials. Remember, our verse says that we are to "know how to answer *everyone*" (Colossians 4:6). The tool or answer that is appropriate for one is not effective for another. Actively seek the Holy Spirit's guidance as to the appropriate tool for them.

Keith was attending a weeklong law enforcement training conference. Back at the motel, he started a conversation with John, another participant. Even though they had just met, John began revealing his heart to Keith. "Sometimes I go out at night and sit on the porch at home. My wife thinks I am just going out for a cigarette. But really I go out to look at the stars and think about God." Three thousand miles away from home, God had opened a door for the message between two men at work.

Give Books, Magazines, or Tapes to Persuade

Once a spiritual conversation has taken place, it can be easy to follow up with books, magazines, or tapes meant to persuade an unbeliever. There are some excellent resources available to give to another person. As you give them to your friend, be honest about the contents of the resource.

More Than a Carpenter, by Josh McDowell, is a thin and understandable book that builds credibility with its proclamation of "10 million sold" on the front. *The Case for Christ,* by Lee Strobel, is a fast-moving record of interviews with expert Christians who prove the truth of Christianity. *The Case for Faith* by the same author answers many of the hard questions unbelievers have with a similar style. *Mere Christianity* by C. S. Lewis is a classic beginning book for the person with an intellectual bent. Check out more resources at www.tonguetied.org.

A week after I had my first spiritual conversation with Frank, I found out he had taken another job. I wanted to put something into his hands, but what? And how? I prayed, and the Lord opened a natural door the day before he left. I referenced the conversation we had several weeks earlier and then gave him *More Than a Carpenter.* Through that conversation, the Lord had made an opportunity for me to put a persuasive book in his hand.

Besides books aimed at unbelievers, some people can enjoy resources aimed at believers. Our neighbors are crusty, independent New Englanders. Though they know we are "religious," it does not interest them. But the husband does read novels. So, after reading the latest *Left Behind* novel, we loaned it to him. With a smile he told us, "You are not going to convert me." With a smile we replied, "That's God's job." The devotional help *Our Daily Bread* can also be used in a similar manner. The stories are attractive to believers and unbelievers alike. And once a month, there is a salvation message. It is available from Radio Bible Class.

If the Lord opens a door for a conversation, we want to have good questions to ask. And we want to have good answers. Part of having those good answers is putting a resource in the person's hands for later. As much as possible, this resource should reflect your personal knowledge of them and where they are in their spiritual journey. Seek the Holy Spirit's guidance as to the appropriate book, tape, or magazine.

Use the Internet

In addition, don't forget the Internet. The amount of information available on the Internet is increasing exponentially. There are answers to any question your friends have. Familiarize yourself with good web sites. Then when a subject comes up, you can suggest a web site name for them to look at. Better yet, you could print out the information and hand it to them. Check out www.tonguetied.org for some of the best sites.

You could also invite them to visit your church's web site. In this day and age, it is not difficult for even small churches to have a web site. A church web site should have a section specifically devoted to those who have questions. Include the conversion stories of real people in your church. See www.tonguetied.org for some links to church sites that do this. Remember, evangelism is personal. This part of the web site is for you to direct your inquiring friends to. They probably will look at it just out of curiosity, even if they never set foot in the door of your fellowship.

Give Resources That Help with a Problem

If we build genuine relationships with unbelievers, they are going to reveal problems they are facing. In addition to an offer of prayer, there is probably an appropriate book, magazine, or teaching tape addressing their problem from a Christian perspective.

Depending on the circumstance, you can either give or loan the resource to them. Loaning has the advantage of giving them a deadline by when they should have used it. When it comes time to collect your loaned resource, you have a natural opportunity to bring up the subject again. Giving someone a book or tape, however, shows love. You took time to think of them, and you spent money for a gift. Marriage issues, parenting issues, and suffering are common areas of concern.

Follow Up with a Personal Letter

A special note that follows a serious conversation makes an additional impact. Composing and sending a personal letter communicates a powerful message of love and concern. It is an especially helpful resource for the tongue-tied. Often, we think of what we should have said or the resource we should have recommended only after the conversation is over. Unfortunately, it may be months before we will see the person again.

If this is the case, write a personal note. Tell the person how much you enjoyed talking with him or her. Perhaps you need to clarify some things you should have said differently. Include a follow-up article or resource that speaks to the person's current need. Be gracious and sincere. And don't procrastinate. Be sure to act while the conversation is fresh in their mind.

Your Family's Fellowship

One of the most powerful evangelistic tools we can have is a loving family. All people desire loving family relationships. Yet sin attacks our relationships with others, and the family—with our closest relationships—is most affected by our sin. Likewise, it is most affected by our godliness.

A loving family and a loving church are naturally attractive to unbelievers. In fact, sometimes the love experienced by unbelievers can run around their heads and go straight for their hearts. In the book *Living Proof,* Jim Petersen talks about working with an argumentative intellectual who finally gave his life to Christ after four years of work. When asked what finally had led him to follow Christ, Jim naturally thought of all the hours invested in conversation.

> His reply took me completely by surprise. He said, "Remember that first time I stopped by your house? We were on our way someplace together, and I had a bowl of soup with you and your family. As I sat there observing you, your wife, your children, and how you related to each other, I asked myself, 'When will I have a relationship like this with my fiancée?' When I realized that the answer was 'never,' I concluded I had to become a Christian for the sake of my own survival."[11]

Was the word preached? Yes. What convinced him? Being in Jim's home and seeing loving relationships.

If appropriate, show love to your friends by inviting them to your house for a meal or including them in some family activity. Don't wait until your family is perfect. They never will be. In fact, Jim recalls that his children were not particularly well behaved on that momentous day. A perfect family is not attractive. A loving one is.

Invite Them to Your Church Fellowship

Even if you are so tongue-tied you cannot envision yourself using any of the resources above, you can end a spiritual conversation by inviting the person to church. If God has already been at work in his or her heart, that will be enough. Andrew brought Peter to meet Jesus, and Peter became the leader of the apostles.

A loving church is similar to a loving family. The supernatural love and unity can be persuasive to an unbeliever. Jesus promised, "By this all men will know you are my disciples, if you love one another" (John 13:35). Sin brings loneliness, emptiness, and joylessness. Conversely, a good church is a place of fellowship, fulfillment, and joy.

Your church is the easiest resource to offer, but it is the hardest for unbelievers to take advantage of. For unbelievers to begin attending church on Sunday, they must overcome several barriers. First, they must wake up early on Sunday morning. Up until now they've been used to sleeping in. Second, they think they have to dress up. Third, if they have children, they will have to wake the children up and have them dressed nicely. Fourth, they will have to meet new people. Entering a room with all new people makes anyone nervous. Given all these barriers, we should be thankful that unbelievers even consider coming to church.

As the Lord leads you, invite people to come to your church. But understand the barriers in their minds. And don't be satisfied with invitations alone. Start here if necessary. But begin to learn how to bring the good news to people. After all, Jesus sent his disciples *to bring* the good news *to* the world (John 20:21). Those who had been scattered preached the word wherever they *went* (Acts 8:4).

Follow Through

God has been pleased to bless these resources in the past. He tells us, "Always be prepared to give an answer to everyone who asks you to give the reason for the hope that you have" (1 Peter 3:15). But nothing says we must have all those answers in our head. God has given evangelists to equip the rest of us for works of service (Ephesians 4:11–12). We would be foolish not to use the resources that they have given to the church.

These resources are like seed. The farmer who is going to sow the field has to invest money to buy the seed. He does so, knowing that some of the seed will be eaten by the birds, and some of the seed will fall on rocky or thorny soil. But the seed that falls on the good soil will produce a return that will more than make up for the wasted seed. The law of the harvest is true: "Whoever sows sparingly will also reap sparingly, and whoever sows generously will also reap generously" (2 Corinthians 9:6). I want to be one who sows generously. Don't you?

For Thought, Discussion, and Action

- How many evangelistic resources do you have in your house? Have you ever used a pamphlet to help you explain the gospel? Is this a good resource for you? Why or why not? Order a package of the pamphlets and ask the Lord to open a door to give one out. See www.tonguetied.org for ordering details.
- Have you ever held a one-to-one evangelistic Bible study? What fears do you have? What benefits can you see to this method? Order several of the one-on-one Bible study resources. Go through one by yourself first.
- Who do you know that might benefit from a book like *More Than a Carpenter*? Order several copies of *More Than a Carpenter*, *The Case for Christ*, or some other resource that seems appropriate. Be sure to read it before giving it to others. See www.tonguetied.org for links to these and other books.
- Have unbelieving friends confided to you about a problem they are having? Is there a resource that might encourage or equip them to handle this problem better? Would you buy it and give it to them?
- Have you had a recent conversation that you need to follow up with? How do you plan to do it?
- When was the last time you had a non-Christian in your home for the purpose of showing the love of Christ? What barriers

stop you? Should they? What can you do about them? Would you pray for an opportunity?

- When was the last time you invited someone to your church? What barriers stop you? Should they? What can you do about them? Would you begin praying for that opportunity?

CHAPTER 10

Staying on Track

I love shooting basketball with my sons on a hot summer evening. The three of us will never play for the National Basketball Association, but we can still have an enjoyable time. In a similar manner, you may never be an evangelistic superstar. But you can enjoy evangelism just like the pros. By understanding and mastering just a few basic skills, you can have the privilege of talking to others about Jesus.

First, *pray biblical evangelistic prayers.* Pray that God would open a door for the message. In addition, pray that you would declare the gospel clearly and fearlessly. Also, pray obstinately, devoting yourself to making smaller requests that will result in regular answers.

Second, *build genuine relationships with unbelievers as you go throughout your day.* Treat each person you meet in a day wisely, as a person made in the image of God. Be alert to the people God brings across your path. Don't force the door open, but be ready when God does make an opportunity.

Third, *transition to spiritual things, using a prepared question.* Use the subject of religion to transition to spiritual things. Or share a story of God working in your life. Have some fun finding out what they believe. Who do they think Jesus is? Ask lots of questions before you speak.

Fourth, *use a resource that God has blessed in the past.* Ask them if they would be interested in reading a pamphlet or having a Bible study. Invite them to your church or to your home, if appropriate. Give a resource that fits them.

That's it. Pretty simple, really. Perhaps you have been a Christian for decades but have forgotten how to talk to others about Jesus. Don't give up in despair. Put these principles into practice, and soon you will be talking to others. As a result, *you* will be blessed. Witnessing really is the fizz of the Christian life, putting sparkle in your walk with the Lord.

Life in the twenty-first century is hurried and only becoming faster. You are to be congratulated for reading this far. But will you take the next step and actually put these principles into practice? It will take courage, perseverance, and a commitment to change. It will not be easy. God desires to use you and will if you are committed to growth. The following suggestions will help in that personal change.

Real Change Takes Others

If you are serious about real, lasting life-change, then you must find at least one or two others to join with you. We need each other to stay on track. You will not be able to do it alone. Jesus taught the principle of teamwork. He sent his disciples out two-by-two for mutual support. Paul understood his need for others, taking Barnabas and Mark on his first journey and Silas and Timothy on his second.

We need others to sharpen us and to encourage us. "As iron sharpens iron, so one man sharpens another" (Proverbs 27:17). We all have blind spots and need the exhortation and challenge of others. Ministry partners can also encourage us. Just as dangerous as ignorance is discouragement. "A cord of three strands is not easily broken" (Ecclesiastes 4:12). Many things vie for our attention. The only way we can progress in this area is by joining with other like-minded individuals. Many times when we speak for Christ, we will experience rejection. Friends can help us persevere.

Your little group can be as formal or as informal as you like. Perhaps you could use an existing small group like your Sunday school class or your mid-week small group. Order a copy of this book for each participant and your pastor. Discuss one chapter a week, using the questions at the end of each chapter. Spend time praying for one another and reporting on victories and problems. Invite the input and advice of others in your group. Be sure to ask your spiritual leaders for their insight as well. You don't need to be a leader or expert. Just be the facilitator for gathering together.

If you cannot persuade an existing group to begin studying and discussing the material, then perhaps there are one or two others in your fellowship who would be interested. Meet once a week to pray for each other, discuss the material and share insights.

Real Change Takes Time

In addition, any lasting change must be processed over time. It has been said that it takes three weeks to form a habit and another three weeks to make that habit part of your life. To produce real change, make a commitment to meet weekly for a short time, like three months. And see what the Lord might do through you in that time frame.

Good intentions are just that—good intentions—until we put some accountability behind it. Everyone needs that accountability. Will you gather some friends together?

Keep a Notebook

Another way to continue learning is to record each spiritual conversation in a notebook. Write down the factors that led you into the conversation and the flow of the conversation. What did you say, and what did the other person say? What were the key questions that started the conversation? What were the key questions that turned the conversation to spiritual things? Write down positive lessons learned and problems you had. Rejoice in the victories.

View the problems as action points on which to work. Did someone ask you a question you did not know how to answer? Write it down, and then find out the answer. Did the conversation die and abruptly turn to other subjects? Think about why it happened and what you could have done differently. What could you ask in the future? Remember, we who are tongue-tied need to have our questions thought out ahead of time. By writing down the flow of the conversation, you will be able to record your progress and your action points. Each conversation I have is a learning experience. I analyze what I did well and what needs improvement. Many of the lessons presented here were mistakes first and victories later. "The wisdom of the prudent is to give thought to their ways" (Proverbs 14:8).

Find All the Training You Can

Remember that evangelism is a set of skills that can be learned with the help of the Holy Spirit. David said, "Praise be to the Lord my Rock, who *trains* my hand for war, my fingers for battle" (Psalm 144:1). We need to take advantage of all the equipping we can. Training is the difference between just fighting and fighting well. The following are several suggestions for further training.

Invite a trusted friend to critique you on how skillful you are at asking good questions and listening to the answers. Listen to his or her response carefully. We talk about ourselves more than we realize. Many times when another person is speaking, we are not really listening but merely pausing until it is our turn to talk.

Learn common objections that unbelievers have and the answers to those objections. Don't be overly concerned about memorizing the answers beforehand. Often that study is forgotten in the midst of the battle. Unfortunately, too much of our training gives us answers that we promptly forget instead of teaching us where to find the answers. Often, the best time to learn an answer is *after* someone has asked us the question. Many of the resources listed in appendix A have excellent sections on how to respond to various objections.

If you are asked a question and don't know the answer, don't panic. Calmly respond, "That's a good question. I don't know the answer, but I will find out." And then find out. Now you have an excuse to have another conversation or to send the answer in a letter. Just remember that while some ask questions out of genuine concern, others use questions as diversionary tactics. In your conversation, attempt to discern whether this person is truly concerned over the issue or whether it is simply to change the direction of the conversation.

Become a student of adult conversion. Interview those around you who became Christians as adults. What were they thinking before they became Christians? What caused them to change? What was attractive about becoming a Christian? The more you ask questions, the more you will understand how God works in the lives of pre-Christians. You will be amazed at the varied means that God uses to reach people. And you will grow in your trust of God. You will realize that the kingdom of God is like a man who scatters seed on the ground.

"Night and day, whether he sleeps or gets up, the seed sprouts and grows, though he does not know how. *All by itself* the soil produces grain—first the stalk, then the head, then the full kernel in the head." (Mark 4:27–28)

We are to scatter, but the life is in the seed. It grows even as we sleep.

Trust God with the Results

Trusting God with the results is one of the hardest lessons to learn. Over and over again, I have become disappointed because I wanted to see immediate results. I wanted to harvest where I have not sown. It is easy to forget that the Word must be sown first, and then the harvest will come. In many, many circumstances there must be a passage of time between the first sowing and the harvest. We cannot rush the harvest. The farmer does his part in sowing the seed. Then he trusts God to do his part in growing the seed.

One summer our church saw several adults give their hearts to the Lord. One was Chris, mentioned above, who had been in a home Bible study but only two years later prayed to receive Christ. I was given the privilege of seeing both the sowing and the harvesting.

Greg also became a Christian that day. But Greg showed up at our church because of a teacher on the radio. This gentleman had helped Greg realize he needed to be saved. He showed up at our church, on the other side of the country, because both the teacher's church and our church ended with the words *Christian Fellowship*. Greg wrongly concluded that we must be part of the same denomination. Regardless, he and his wife prayed to receive Christ the same day as Chris. That radio teacher will not know that his proclamation bore fruit until Greg meets him in heaven.

Similarly, much of our fruit will be hidden from us. We need to trust God with the results. Focus on sowing the Word and making the mystery of Christ clear. If we do that, God will bless us. He promises that if we sow abundantly, we will reap abundantly (2 Corinthians 9:6).

Have Fun

Related to trusting God with the results is an attitude of having fun. Remember, we are not gifted in this area! We are just out discovering what people believe, and we are sowing the Word. As we go throughout our day, we are looking for those serendipitous moments when God opens a door for the message.

We are going to find ourselves in some dead ends. There will be times when we do not know what to say. We are going to be fearful and not speak up once or twice. Relax! God is control. God is the one who gives salvation, not you. The person's eternal destiny depends on God and them, not on you saying the right words at the right time. You are not the important one.

Evangelism is fun. Every time we engage a person in talking about spiritual things, it's a victory. With your help, they thought about eternity for a moment. That's a triumph. They know you are a Christian. That's success. And if you made the mystery of Christ clear, then that's a victory too. Relax and have fun.

I recently received this note from a member of our church.

> I'm flying kind of high tonight. I just got home from my fiftieth class reunion. I told the Lord I would take any opportunities to witness he would give me. I ended up "preaching" to a table full and particularly a husband and wife. It was one of the most exciting times I have ever had sharing the gospel. The wife took my phone number and is going to call me, and they both want me to come to their home to tell them more. They were extremely receptive. I went to this event, not with a superior attitude, but with confidence that I was a child of the King and I was richer than anyone there. Because of that, I longed to have each one experience peace that only he can give.

That can be you. You also can experience the same joy of telling others about Christ. When God uses you, encourage others with what is happening in you and through you. Be sure to send me your encouraging stories by e-mail to stories@tonguetied.org. Let me share in your joy!

> Now to him who is able to do *immeasurably more than all we ask or imagine*, according to his power that is at work within us, to him be glory in the church and in Christ Jesus throughout all generations, for ever and ever! Amen. (Ephesians 3:20–21)

APPENDIX A

Resources

Unless another supplier is listed, all resources are available at www.tonguetied.org or through your local Christian bookstore.

Resources to Encourage Your Prayers

Pray the Lord's Prayer for Your Neighbors. A twenty-eight-day devotional guide that helps you learn to pray the Lord's Prayer for yourself and your neighbors. Each day has a Bible passage, meditation, and prayer suggestions. Helps focus and vary your evangelistic prayers. Order from Houses of Prayer Everywhere (800–217–5200).

Developing a Prayer-Care-Share Lifestyle. The three sections of this book, containing five weeks of five readings each, will help you (1) grow in prayer, (2) reach out with care, and (3) sensitively share the blessings of Christ with those around you. It is another resource to help focus your evangelistic prayers. Order from Houses of Prayer Everywhere.

Pamphlets That Help You Explain the Gospel

Steps to Peace with God. A colorful gospel pamphlet from the Billy Graham Evangelistic Association. One of my favorites.

The Four Spiritual Laws. The gospel pamphlet used by Campus Crusade for Christ. Over 100 million copies have been printed. Available for viewing online in English and many other languages. Variations of this pamphlet include:

- *Would You Like to Know God Personally?* Uses the concept of four spiritual principles instead of laws.
- *Would You Like to Belong to God's Family?* Aimed at children in grade school.
- *Beginning Your Journey of Joy.* Designed for women to share with other women.
- *Connecting with God.* Targets today's high school and college students.

Links to view or order these gospel resources are available online at the web site listed above, which also has links to many excellent sites on the subject.

Resources to Help You Lead a Bible Study

Knowing Jesus Christ. Book 1 of the Studies in Christian Living series from NavPress. Excellent for one-to-one Bible studies. Three studies: "Who Is Jesus Christ?"; "The Work of Jesus Christ"; and "Eternal Life in Jesus Christ."

Who Is This Jesus? A twelve-page evangelistic handout that can be used for one-to-one Bible study. Five short studies on Jesus as healer, teacher, redeemer, and life-giver. Order from Campus Crusade (800–827–2788).

Your Home a Lighthouse. Step-by-step instructions on how to lead a once-a-month home Bible study for non-Christians. The appendix has discussion questions for each chapter of John. Aimed at leading a group study.

Books to Read and Give to a Non-Christian

More Than a Carpenter. Over ten million copies of this persuasive book are in print. Josh McDowell answers questions that show that Jesus was more than just a carpenter. Small enough so as not to be overwhelming but still comprehensive.

The Case for Christ. Lee Strobel takes the reader through gripping interviews with experts in the field of psychology, forensics, history, and other areas to prove the case for Jesus Christ being who he claimed to be. Thick but engaging.

The Case for Faith. Lee Strobel investigates the tough objections to Christianity: How can a loving God allow evil and suffering? How can miracles be true? How can a loving God torture his creatures in hell? As above, a thick book but still engaging. Not quite as conservative as it could be but still excellent.

Mere Christianity. C. S. Lewis's classic work defending the essentials of ("mere") Christianity. For the person with an intellectual orientation.

One Minute after You Die. Erwin Lutzer writes on the realities of the afterlife and what one can expect in heaven or hell. More readable than the previous books.

Web Sites to Read and Give to Non-Christians

See www.tonguetied.org for a constantly updated list of recommended web sites to read and give to the non-Christian.

Books to Equip Christians for Evangelism

The first five books are excellent supplements to *Evangelism for the Tongue-Tied.*

How to Give Away Your Faith. This classic by Paul Little will encourage you to be friendly and natural when sharing your faith. Over a million copies have been sold. Aimed particularly at the college student but helpful for all.

Out of the Salt Shaker. Becky Pippert is at her best when she is helping us relax, be open, and be honest as we tell others about Jesus. There are also practical chapters on how to share in a conversational style. Also aimed at the college student but helpful to all.

Witnessing without Fear. Authored by Bill Bright, founder of Campus Crusade. Helpful chapters on overcoming fear and keeping the gospel simple. Encouraging and plainly written. Don't let all the author's successes intimidate you.

Share Jesus without Fear. Excellent questions and tips for sharing the gospel with someone. William Fay's style is difficult for the tongue-tied Christian to imitate, but we can learn from his lists of questions and responses.

How to Talk about Jesus without Freaking Out. A thorough guide-book using principles the authors have learned in one of the most secular places in the world—Hollywood.

Your Home a Lighthouse. This practical handbook will help you host an evangelistic Bible study in your home or anywhere else. Helpful for those who have relationships but don't know what to do next.

Divine Appointments. Great stories about viewing your day as a chance to have divine, Holy Spirit-guided appointments. Illustrates building genuine relationships as you go about your day, ready for the Holy Spirit to open a door for the message.

Conspiracy of Kindness. A simple approach for a church group to reach out through acts of kindness, overcoming barriers of cynical people. Our church has used some of these principles to building genuine relationships in a deliberate way.

Lifestyle Evangelism. Joe Aldrich explains how to be the kind of people who attract others to Jesus by their lifestyles, showing readers how to establish common ground with the unsaved, build relationships, and live lives that exemplify the character of Jesus. If you need help with building genuine relationships, this book is for you.

Books to Equip, Which Discuss the Reasons for the Faith

Know Why You Believe. Paul Little gives Christians a readable book on answers to common questions believers and unbelievers have. Examples include: Is there a God? Did Christ rise from the dead? Why does God allow evil and suffering? More complete answers than in *How to Give Away Your Faith.*

Evidence that Demands a Verdict. Josh McDowell exhaustively lists all the evidence for the truth of Christianity. *The* apologetic reference book to have.

Handbook of Today's Religions. Josh McDowell gives us a reference book for the major beliefs for the different religions active in the United States. This work should be in every church and pastor's library.

Web Sites to Equip Christians for Evangelism

See www.tonguetied.org for a constantly updated list of recommended web sites to better equip you for evangelism.

Conversion, Convincing, and Coping Stories

Visit www.tonguetied.org and download the free worksheet, which has room for you to write out your story.

Biblical Examples

The blind man: "Whether he is a sinner or not, I don't know. One thing I do know. *I was blind but now I see*" (John 9:25).

The demoniac: "As Jesus was getting into the boat, the man who had been demon-possessed begged to go with him. Jesus did not let him but said, 'Go home and *tell your family how much the Lord has done for you* and how he has had mercy on you.' So the man went away and began to tell in Decapolis how much Jesus had done for him. And all the people were amazed" (Mark 5:18–20).

The Samaritan woman: "Many of the Samaritans from that town believed in him *because of the woman's testimony*" (John 4:39).

The apostle Paul: to the Jews (Acts 22:1–21), to Agrippa (26:2–23).

Dos and Don'ts
- Do keep it short and sweet (about three minutes).
- Do break it into three parts: B.C. (Before Christ), R.C. (Receiving Christ), A.D. (After Christ.)

- Do spend the most time on the benefits in your life A.D.
- Do use a Bible verse directly related to your story.
- Do be realistic.
- Don't exaggerate.
- Do be specific about your life B.C. and A.D.
- Do keep unbelievers in mind as you write it out.
- Don't use vague terms and Christian lingo (such as *saved, blessing, ways of the world*).
- Don't attack any church or denomination.
- Don't include irrelevant detail.
- Do write out the talking points you want to remember.

Questions to Help with the Story of Your Conversion

Describe your life before you received Christ.

- What were your attitudes, needs, and problems before you received Christ?
- What did your life revolve around?
- What were you doing for happiness and security?
- How was this life unfulfilling?
- How did you realize that it was unfulfilling?

Here are some words that might describe your situation and thinking:

inner emptiness	purposelessness
fear of death	bitterness
sense of guilt	sense of dirtiness
desire for inner peace	loneliness
lack of truth	lack of self-control
general hopelessness	marriage problems
self-centeredness	

Describe how you received Christ.

- When did you first hear about a relationship with Christ?
- What was your reaction?
- Why did you change your mind? What happened?
- Did any verse stick in your mind during this time?

Describe your life after you received Christ.

- How has your life changed since you received Christ?
- How is your life better now that you have received Christ?

Here are some words to prime your thinking on the benefits you have received in Christ:

clear conscience	purpose
inner peace	new confidence
inner security	fulfillment
freedom,	eternal life
victory over sin	ability to forgive others
sense of God's forgiveness	new concern for others
desire to read the Bible	new love for God
the power to change	power and strength
help with weakness	new attitudes
new awareness of sin	benefits to my marriage
new concern for others	benefits to my children

Questions to Help with the Story of Your Convincing

Describe your life before you came back to Christ.

- What were your attitudes, needs, and problems?
- What did your life revolve around?
- What were you doing for happiness and security?
- How was this unfulfilling?
- How did you realize that it was unfulfilling?

Here are some words that might describe your situation and thinking at that time:

inner emptiness	purposelessness
fear of death	bitterness
sense of guilt	sense of dirtiness
desire for inner peace	loneliness
lack of truth	lack of self-control
general hopelessness	marriage problems
self-centeredness	

Describe how you became convinced of following Jesus.

- How did God begin to work to bring you back?
- What thoughts were you having that began to change your mind?
- What convinced you to change your mind? What happened?
- Did any verse stick in your mind during this time?

Describe your life after you committed your life to follow Christ.

- How has your life changed?
- How is your life better now?

Here are some words to prime your thinking on the benefits of committing your life to following Christ:

clear conscience	purpose
inner peace	new confidence
inner security	fulfillment
freedom	eternal life
victory over sin	ability to forgive others
sense of God's forgiveness	new concern for others
desire to read the Bible	new love for God
the power to change	power and strength
help with weakness	new attitudes
new awareness of sin	benefits to my marriage
new concern for others	benefits to my children

Questions to Help with Your Coping Stories

Describe the crisis or stress in your life. Here are some types of problems to prime your thinking:

marital problems	losing a child to death
financial problems	parenting problems
dating betrayal	friendship betrayal
work problems	addiction problems
severe health problems	moving stress
infertility	depression

an accident   stress from a new baby
stress from a promotion

Or: stress from dealing with someone who has one of the above problems.

Describe how knowing Jesus helped you cope with that hard time.

- How did you handle the problem?
- How would you have handled the problem before you were a Christian?
- What practical difference did it make that you had the Lord during that time?
- Did any verse stick in your mind during this time?

Questions to Help You Refine and Use Your Stories

- Did you write it out?
- Does it flow logically?
- Did you follow the dos and don'ts above?
- Is it relatively brief and to the point, so that it will fit in a conversation?
- Have you practiced it with a friend and spiritual leader to hear their feedback?
- Have you written talking points some place where you will see them regularly, like the flyleaf of your Bible?

Notes

[1] Paul Little, *How to Give Away Your Faith* (Downers Grove, Ill.: InterVarsity, 1988), 36.

[2] Joe Aldrich, *Lifestyle Evangelism* (Sisters, Oreg: Multnomah, 1993), 53.

[3] *Webster's New International Dictionary*, 3rd ed., s.v. "tongue-tied."

[4] C. S. Lewis, *The Weight of Glory and Other Addresses* (New York: Macmillan, 1949), 14–15.

[5] J. I. Packer, *Evangelism and the Sovereignty of God* (Downers Grove, Ill.: InterVarsity, 1961), 27.

[6] Michael Horton, *Putting Amazing Back into Grace* (Grand Rapids: Baker, 1994), 101.

[7] Alan Wolfe, *One Nation, After All* (New York: Viking, 1998), 233.

[8] Paul Little, *How to Give Away Your Faith* (Downers Grove, Ill.: InterVarsity, 1988), 67.

[9] John Powell, *Why Am I Afraid to Tell You Who I Am?* (Niles, Ill.: Argus Communications, 1969), 54–62.

[10] William Fay, *Share Jesus without Fear* (Nashville: Broadman & Holman, 1999), 34–35.

[11] Jim Petersen, *Living Proof* (Colorado Springs: NavPress, 1989), 119.

To order additional copies of

Evangelism
for the
Tongue-Tied

Visit your local book store

or call 1-877-421-READ (7323)

Or order online at www.pleasantword.com

Also available at:
www.amazon.com
www.barnesandnoble.com
and
www.christianbook.com

For more evangelistic resources
or to contact the author
visit
www.tonguetied.org

Printed in the United States
24897LVS00004B/385-429